Dreamweaver 8.
Basic
Student Manual

Serius Web Solutions

Kith Graham

597-1707

THOMSON
━━━━━━━━━━✴━━━━━━━━━━™
COURSE TECHNOLOGY

Australia • Canada • Mexico • Singapore
Spain • United Kingdom • United States

Dreamweaver 8: Basic

VP and GM, Training Group:	Michael Springer
Series Product Managers:	Charles G. Blum and Adam A. Wilcox
Developmental Editor:	Brandon Heffernan
Copyeditor:	Catherine Oliver
Keytester:	Cliff Coryea
Series Designer:	Adam A. Wilcox
Cover Designer:	Steve Deschene

For more information contact:

Course Technology
25 Thomson Place
Boston, MA 02210

Or find us on the Web at: www.course.com

For permission to use material from this text or product, submit a request online at: www.thomsonrights.com

Any additional questions about permissions can be submitted by e-mail to: thomsonrights@thomson.com

Trademarks
Course ILT is a trademark of Course Technology.

Some of the product names and company names used in this book have been used for identification purposes only and may be trademarks or registered trademarks of their respective manufacturers and sellers.

Disclaimer
Course Technology reserves the right to revise this publication and make changes from time to time in its content without notice.

ISBNs

    1-4188-8985-7 = Student Manual

    1-4188-8987-3 = Student Manual with data CD

Printed in the United States of America

1 2 3 4 5 6 7 8 9 PM 08 07 06

Contents

Introduction

After reading this introduction, you will know how to:

A Use Course Technology ILT manuals in general.

B Use prerequisites, a target student description, course objectives, and a skills inventory to properly set your expectations for the course.

C Re-key this course after class.

Topic A: About the manual

Course Technology ILT philosophy

Course Technology ILT manuals facilitate your learning by providing structured interaction with the software itself. While we provide text to explain difficult concepts, the hands-on activities are the focus of our courses. By paying close attention as your instructor leads you through these activities, you will learn the skills and concepts effectively.

We believe strongly in the instructor-led classroom. During class, focus on your instructor. Our manuals are designed and written to facilitate your interaction with your instructor, and not to call attention to manuals themselves.

We believe in the basic approach of setting expectations, delivering instruction, and providing summary and review afterwards. For this reason, lessons begin with objectives and end with summaries. We also provide overall course objectives and a course summary to provide both an introduction to and closure on the entire course.

Manual components

The manuals contain these major components:

- Table of contents
- Introduction
- Units
- Course summary
- Quick reference
- Glossary
- Index

Each element is described below.

Table of contents

The table of contents acts as a learning roadmap.

Introduction

The introduction contains information about our training philosophy and our manual components, features, and conventions. It contains target student, prerequisite, objective, and setup information for the specific course.

Units

Units are the largest structural component of the course content. A unit begins with a title page that lists objectives for each major subdivision, or topic, within the unit. Within each topic, conceptual and explanatory information alternates with hands-on activities. Units conclude with a summary comprising one paragraph for each topic, and an independent practice activity that gives you an opportunity to practice the skills you've learned.

The conceptual information takes the form of text paragraphs, exhibits, lists, and tables. The activities are structured in two columns, one telling you what to do, the other providing explanations, descriptions, and graphics.

Course summary

This section provides a text summary of the entire course. It is useful for providing closure at the end of the course. The course summary also indicates the next course in this series, if there is one, and lists additional resources you might find useful as you continue to learn about the software.

Quick reference

The quick reference is an at-a-glance job aid summarizing some of the more common features of the software.

Glossary

The glossary provides definitions for all of the key terms used in this course.

Index

The index at the end of this manual makes it easy for you to find information about a particular software component, feature, or concept.

Manual conventions

We've tried to keep the number of elements and the types of formatting to a minimum in the manuals. This aids in clarity and makes the manuals more classically elegant looking. But there are some conventions and icons you should know about.

Convention	Description
Italic text	In conceptual text, indicates a new term or feature.
Bold text	In unit summaries, indicates a key term or concept. In an independent practice activity, indicates an explicit item that you select, choose, or type.
`Code font`	Indicates code or syntax.

`Longer strings of ►`
`    code will look ►`
`    like this.`
	In the hands-on activities, any code that's too long to fit on a single line is divided into segments by one or more continuation characters (►). This code should be entered as a continuous string of text.

Select **bold item**	In the left column of hands-on activities, bold sans-serif text indicates an explicit item that you select, choose, or type.
Keycaps like (↵ ENTER)	Indicate a key on the keyboard you must press.

Hands-on activities

The hands-on activities are the most important parts of our manuals. They are divided into two primary columns. The "Here's how" column gives short instructions to you about what to do. The "Here's why" column provides explanations, graphics, and clarifications. Here's a sample:

Do it!

A-1: Creating a commission formula

Here's how	Here's why
1 Open Sales	This is an oversimplified sales compensation worksheet. It shows sales totals, commissions, and incentives for five sales reps.
2 Observe the contents of cell F4	F4 ▼ = =E4*C_Rate
	The commission rate formulas use the name "C_Rate" instead of a value for the commission rate.

For these activities, we have provided a collection of data files designed to help you learn each skill in a real-world business context. As you work through the activities, you will modify and update these files. Of course, you might make a mistake and, therefore, want to re-key the activity starting from scratch. To make it easy to start over, you will rename each data file at the end of the first activity in which the file is modified. Our convention for renaming files is to add the word "My" to the beginning of the file name. In the above activity, for example, a file called "Sales" is being used for the first time. At the end of this activity, you would save the file as "My sales," thus leaving the "Sales" file unchanged. If you make a mistake, you can start over using the original "Sales" file.

In some activities, however, it may not be practical to rename the data file. If you want to retry one of these activities, ask your instructor for a fresh copy of the original data file.

Topic B: Setting your expectations

Properly setting your expectations is essential to your success. This topic will help you do that by providing:

- Prerequisites for this course
- A description of the target student at whom the course is aimed
- A list of the objectives for the course
- A skills assessment for the course

Course prerequisites

Before taking this course, you should be familiar with personal computers and the use of a keyboard and a mouse. Furthermore, this course assumes that you've completed the following courses or have equivalent experience:

- *Windows 2000: Basic* or *Windows XP: Basic*

Target student

This course will benefit students who want to learn to use Dreamweaver 8 to create and modify Web sites. You will learn how to format text, apply styles, create tables, manage images and links, manage Web site files, and publish a site. You should be comfortable using a PC and have experience with Microsoft Windows XP or 2000. You should have little or no experience with Dreamweaver.

Course objectives

These overall course objectives will give you an idea about what to expect from the course. It is also possible that they will help you see that this course is not the right one for you. If you think you either lack the prerequisite knowledge or already know most of the subject matter to be covered, you should let your instructor know that you think you are misplaced in the class.

After completing this course, you will know how to:

- Discuss basic Internet and HTML concepts; identify components of the Dreamweaver workspace; edit and format text; and view the HTML code for a Web page.
- Plan and define a Web site; use Map view and the Assets panel to manage a site; create a Web page; import text from other documents; and modify colors and other page properties.
- Create paragraphs and basic page structures; insert special characters; format text by applying HTML tags and list formats; create CSS style sheets; and add style-sheet rules to control the appearance of content.
- Create tables to arrange data and control page layout; set row and column properties; format tables; and use layout tables to design pages.
- Choose appropriate image formats; embed images and set image properties; create appropriate alternate text; and apply background images.

- Create links to other pages and resources; create named anchors, e-mail links, and image maps; and format links with CSS.

- Connect to a Web server through a secure FTP connection; check a site for broken links and orphaned files; and upload a site.

Skills inventory

Use the following form to gauge your skill level entering the class. For each skill listed, rate your familiarity from 1 to 5, with five being the most familiar. *This is not a test.* Rather, it is intended to provide you with an idea of where you're starting from at the beginning of class. If you're wholly unfamiliar with all the skills, you might not be ready for the class. If you think you already understand all of the skills, you might need to move on to the next course in the series. In either case, you should let your instructor know as soon as possible.

Skill	1	2	3	4	5
Identifying Dreamweaver workspace components	✓				
Editing and formatting text	✓				
Viewing HTML code	✓				
Creating a Web site	✓				
Creating a Web page	✓				
Creating paragraphs	✓				
Applying basic page structures	✓				
Inserting special characters	✓				
Creating lists	✓				
Creating CSS style sheets	✓				
Applying font and color styles	✓				
Creating, modifying, and formatting tables	✓				
Designing with layout tables and layout cells	✓				
Embedding images	✓				
Setting image attributes	✓				
Applying background images	✓				
Creating links	✓				
Creating and linking to named anchors	✓				
Creating image maps	✓				

Skill	1	2	3	4	5
Formatting links with CSS					
Connecting to a Web server					

Topic C: Re-keying the course

If you have the proper hardware and software, you can re-key this course after class. This section explains what you'll need in order to do so, and how to do it.

Computer requirements

To re-key this course, your personal computer must have:

- A keyboard and a mouse
- 800 MHz Intel Pentium III processor or higher
- At least 256 MB RAM (1 GB recommended)
- 2.2 GB of hard-disk space
- A CD-ROM drive for installation
- An XGA monitor with 1024×768 resolution and 32-bit color support
- Internet access

Setup instructions to re-key the course

Before you re-key the course, you will need to perform the following steps.

1   Install Windows XP Professional on an NTFS partition according to the software manufacturer's instructions. You can also use Windows 2000 Professional, although the screen shots in this course were taken using Windows XP, so your screens might look somewhat different.

2   Install Macromedia Dreamweaver 8 according to the software manufacturer's instructions.

3   Install Microsoft Office 2000, XP, or 2003 according to the software manufacturer's instructions. Accept all defaults during installation. (This is required to complete Activity B-2 in the "Web sites and pages" unit.)

4   If necessary, reset any defaults that you have changed. If you do not wish to reset the defaults, you can still re-key the course, but some activities might not work exactly as documented.

5   Adjust the computer's display settings as follows:

    a   Right-click the desktop and choose Properties to open the Display Properties dialog box.

    b   On the Settings tab, change the Color quality to 16 bit or higher and the Screen resolution to 1024 by 768 pixels. (If your monitor is small, consider using a higher screen resolution, if possible.)

    c   On the Appearance tab, set Windows and buttons to Windows XP style.

    d   Click OK. If you are prompted to accept the new settings, click OK and click Yes. Then, if necessary, close the Display Properties dialog box.

6   Adjust Internet properties as follows:

    a   Start Internet Explorer. Choose Tools, Internet Options.

    b   On the General tab, click Use Blank, and click Apply.

    c   On the Advanced tab, under Security, check Allow active content to run in files on My Computer, and click Apply. (This option will appear only if you updated Windows XP with Service Pack 2.)

    d   On the Connections tab, click Setup to start the Internet Connection Wizard.

    e   Click Cancel. A message box appears.

    f   Check "Do not show the Internet Connection wizard in the future," and click Yes.

    g   Close the Internet Options dialog box, and close Internet Explorer.

7   Set up an e-mail account in Microsoft Outlook Express. (You will not actually send or receive messages in this course, so a fully functional e-mail account is not needed.) Without an e-mail client, you will not be able to complete activity A-3 in the Links unit.

    a   Choose Start, All Programs, Outlook Express. (This starts the Internet Connection Wizard for Outlook Express.)

    b   Click Cancel, then Yes to close the Wizard.

8   Display file extensions.

    a   Start Windows Explorer.

    b   Choose Tools, Folder Options and select the View tab.

    c   Clear the check box for Hide extensions for known file types.

    d   Close Windows Explorer.

9   Create a folder called Student Data at the root of the hard drive (C:\).

10 Download the Student Data files for the course.

    a   Connect to www.courseilt.com/instructor_tools.html.

    b   Click the link for Macromedia Dreamweaver to display a page of course listings, and then click the link for Dreamweaver 8: Basic.

    c   Click the link for downloading the student data files, and follow the instructions that appear on your screen.

11 Copy the data files to the Student Data folder.

Unit 1

Getting started

Mozilla—Firebird
www.mozilla.com
used to check syntax

Unit time: 60 minutes

Complete this unit, and you'll know how to:

A Discuss basic Internet and HTML concepts.

B Identify the components of the Dreamweaver 8 workspace.

C Edit and format text on an existing Web page, insert images, and preview a page in a browser.

D View the HTML code of a Web page, and identify the most fundamental HTML tags.

Topic A: Internet basics

Explanation

Before you start using Dreamweaver to design and create Web sites, you should first understand the basics of the Internet, the Web, and HTML.

The Internet and the Web

The *Internet* is a vast array of networks that belong to universities, businesses, organizations, governments, and individuals all over the world. The World Wide Web, or simply *Web*, is one of many services of the Internet. Other Internet services include e-mail, File Transfer Protocol (FTP), and instant messaging.

To view Web pages and other content, you need a Web browser, such as Internet Explorer, Netscape, Safari, or Firefox. Web content typically includes text, images, and multimedia files. Each page or resource has a unique address known as a *Uniform Resource Locater* (URL).

A *Web site* is a collection of linked pages. The top-level page is commonly called the *home page*. A home page typically provides hyperlinks to navigate to other pages within the site or to external pages. A *hyperlink*, or *link* for short, is text or an image that, when clicked, takes the user to another page, another place on the current page, or another Web site.

HTML

Hypertext Markup Language, or *HTML,* is a standard markup language on the Web. HTML enables you to structure and present your Web site's content. An HTML document is a plain text file that contains HTML code, along with the content for a Web page. Exhibit 1-1 shows an example of a simple HTML document. You can create an HTML document by using any text editor, such as Notepad (Windows) or TextEdit (Mac). HTML documents have either an .htm or .html file extension.

HTML code encloses your text content and defines the basic structure of a Web page. A Web page can contain links, references to images, multimedia files, and other elements. When a browser opens a Web page, the text typically loads quickly, while images and embedded media files might take a while longer.

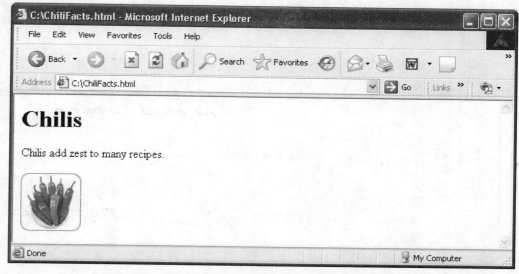

Exhibit 1-1: A simple Web page shown as HTML and in a browser

Do it!

A-1: Discussing the Web and HTML

Questions and answers

1 What's the difference between the Internet and the World Wide Web?

SAME world wide web is one of the internet services.

2 What other Internet services are there?

EMAIL, FTP & messaging

3 What's a Web page?

Each page has a unique URL

4 What's a Web site?

A site has several linked pages

5 What's a Web browser?

6 What is HTML?

Hyper text markup language

Topic B: The Dreamweaver workspace

Explanation

Macromedia Dreamweaver 8 is Web authoring software that helps you design and create Web pages and sites. When you create or change a page in the Dreamweaver workspace, Dreamweaver automatically generates the required HTML, CSS, or scripting code for the page. You can also write or edit the code yourself. Before you start creating Web sites, though, you'll need to be familiar with various components of the Dreamweaver workspace.

Opening files

To open a file in Dreamweaver:

1 Choose Start, All Programs, Macromedia, Macromedia Dreamweaver 8. The Workspace Setup dialog box appears.
2 Verify that Designer is selected, and click OK. The Start page appears, as shown in Exhibit 1-2.
3 Check Don't show again (if you wish), and then click OK.
4 Choose File, Open and browse to locate the file you want to open. Select the file and click Open, or double-click the file.

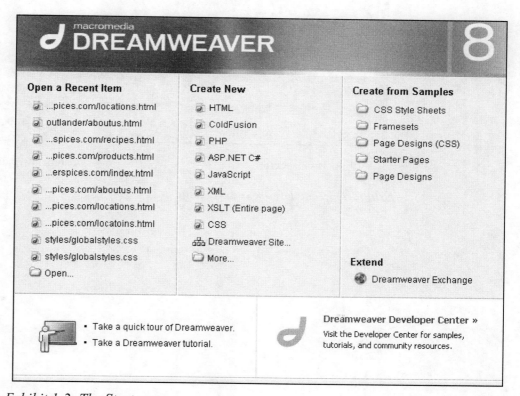

Exhibit 1-2: The Start page

Interface components

As shown in Exhibit 1-3, Dreamweaver's default interface elements include the Insert bar, the Document toolbar, the document window, the Property inspector, and the panel groups.

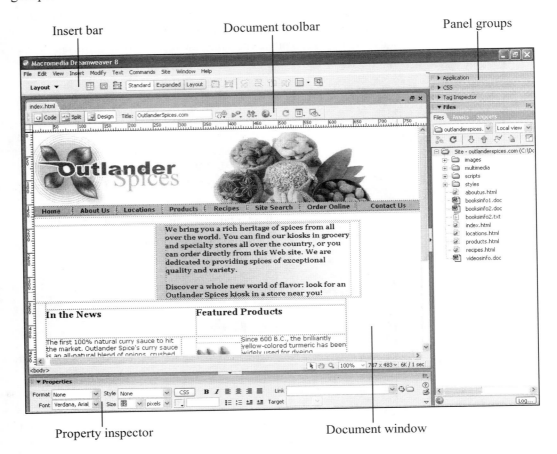

Exhibit 1-3: The Dreamweaver 8 interface

The following table describes the components of the Dreamweaver interface.

Component	Description
Insert bar	Provides buttons you can use to insert objects, such as images, tables, or layers, into a document.
Document toolbar	Provides buttons you can use to perform a variety of tasks. For example, you can switch between Code view, Design view, and Split view, and you can upload files, check for errors, and preview a page in a Web browser.
Panel groups	Is a set of panels you use to change the properties of a Web page. You can access a panel by clicking the panel name. One of the most frequently used is the Files panel group, which displays Web pages and other files, as shown in Exhibit 1-3.
Property inspector	Is a context-sensitive tool that displays the properties of a selected object. You can click the expander arrow in the lower-right corner of the Property inspector to display more options.
Document window	Displays the current Web page.

Do it!

B-1: Identifying Dreamweaver interface components

Here's how	Here's why
1 Choose **Start**, **All Programs**, **Macromedia**, **Macromedia Dreamweaver 8**	To start Dreamweaver 8. The Workspace Setup dialog box appears.
Verify that Designer is selected	
Click **OK**	To use the Designer workspace. The Start page appears.
2 Check **Don't show again**	(To prevent the Start page from appearing whenever Dreamweaver 8 starts.) The Dreamweaver 8 dialog box appears.
Check **Don't show me this message again**	
Click **OK**	
3 Choose **File**, **Open…**	You'll open the index.html Web page.
4 Browse to the current unit folder	
Browse to the outlanderspices.com folder	
Select **index.html**	Home pages are often named index.html because most Web servers are configured to look for that file name as the Web site's "root," or top-level file.
Click **Open**	To open the Outlander Spices home page.
5 Identify the menu bar	The drop-down menus in the menu bar contain commands to perform a wide variety of functions.
6 Identify the Insert bar	The Insert bar provides commands that add elements to a page. The buttons on the Insert bar are shortcuts to the commands in the Insert menu.
7 Identify the Document toolbar	The Document toolbar contains three buttons that control the current view of the open Web page. This toolbar also displays the page title and provides buttons and pop-up menus for frequently used commands.
8 Identify the document window	The document window displays the open Web page.
9 Identify the Property inspector	The Property inspector displays attributes of the selected page element.

10	Identify the Panel groups	The Panel groups enable you to change a variety of Web-page properties.
11	Identify the Files panel	The Files panel displays a list of your files and folders.
12	Choose **View**, **Visual Aids**, **Table Widths**	To remove the table-width indicators that appear by default.

Panel groups

Explanation

Each panel group contains individual panels that are represented by tabs, as shown in Exhibit 1-4. You can use these panels to manage file properties or to manage the properties of elements on the current Web page. The following table describes some of the more commonly used panel groups and the panels they contain.

Panel group	Panels included	Used to...
Files	Files	Manage files and folders.
	Assets	Manage your site *assets*, such as images or multimedia files. To use the Assets panel, you must first define a local site.
	Snippets	Manage *snippets*, which are reusable pieces of HTML code or scripting code.
CSS	CSS Styles	Manage the CSS styles of the selected element. This panel is context-sensitive.
	Layers	Manage layer properties, including overlapping, visibility, and stacking order.
Tag inspector	Attributes	Manage every attribute that can be assigned to an HTML tag.
	Behaviors	Manage JavaScript code. You can insert JavaScript code to create dynamic and interactive page elements.

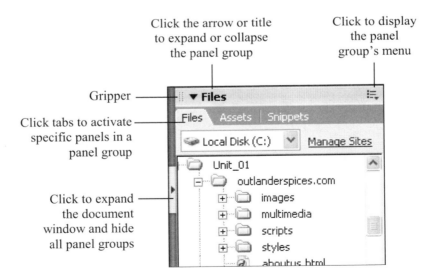

Click the arrow or title to expand or collapse the panel group

Click to display the panel group's menu

Gripper

Click tabs to activate specific panels in a panel group

Click to expand the document window and hide all panel groups

Exhibit 1-4: The Files panel group

You can customize the Dreamweaver workspace by manipulating panel groups as described in the following table.

To do this...	Follow these instructions
Hide or display a panel group	Choose Window and then the name of the panel group.
Expand or collapse a panel group	Click its name in the panel group's title bar.
Move a panel group to a region of the workspace	Drag from the gripper (in the upper-left corner of the panel).
Expand a panel group that has been moved in the workspace	Point to the edge of the panel until the pointer changes to a double-sided arrow, and then drag.
Hide all panel groups and expand the document window	Click the arrow bar between the document window and the panel groups.

Do it!

B-2: Exploring panel groups

Here's how	Here's why
1 Identify the Files panel group	This group lists files and folders. It includes panels for Files, Assets, and Snippets. You can use the Files panel to open or move files.
Click the title, as shown	‖ ▶ Files
	To collapse the panel. You'll explore the other panel groups.
2 Activate the CSS panel group	This group includes the CSS Styles and Layers panels.
Collapse the CSS panel group	Click the title of the CSS panel group.
3 Activate the Application panel group	This group contains the Databases, Bindings, Server Behaviors, and Components panels.
Right-click the title of the Application panel	
Choose **Close Panel Group**	To remove the panel group from the display. The Application panel group contains panels that are not used in this course.
4 Activate the Tag Inspector panel group	The Tag Inspector panel group includes the Attributes and Behaviors panels.
Collapse the panel group	
5 Activate the Files panel group	You'll use the Files panel to display the site files.
In the Files panel, click the Site list and choose **Local Disk (C:)**	To select the root directory of the hard drive. You'll navigate to the current unit folder.
6 Point to the gripper, as shown	‖ ↕ Files Files Assets Snippets
	The pointer changes to a four-sided arrow, indicating that you can move the panel in any direction.
Drag the panel group to the center of the workspace	To undock the panel group from the side of the workspace.

7 Point to the right edge of the new
    panel window, as shown

The pointer changes to a double-sided arrow,
indicating that you can resize the window.

Drag to the right   To enlarge the panel.

8 Navigate to the current unit folder

Drag the Files panel group back to   Drag from the gripper. You can drag the
the other panel groups   window anywhere onto the panel groups to re-
                                                         dock the panel.

9 Next to the panel groups, click   To hide the panel groups and create more space
                                                         in which to work in the document window.
                                                         Notice that the arrow now points outward.
                                                         Clicking the button again will show the panel
                                                         groups.

Click the arrow button again   To display the panel groups.

The Property inspector

Explanation

The Property inspector is context-sensitive. It displays the attributes and properties of the object that is selected in the document window. The expander arrow in the Property inspector's lower-right corner expands or collapses the Property inspector to show or hide additional options.

Do it!

B-3: Working with the Property inspector

Here's how	Here's why
1 In the document window, click **In the News**	You'll use the Property inspector to view the attributes for this text.
2 Observe the Property inspector	The format, font, style, and other attributes of this text are displayed.
Click ▽	(If necessary.) To expand the Property inspector. The Property inspector now includes attributes for the table cell containing the selected text.
3 In the document window, click the image shown	
	(Scroll down if necessary.) To select it.
4 Observe the Property inspector	The Property inspector displays the attributes of the selected image.
Click △	(The expander arrow.) To collapse the Property inspector.
5 Above the Property inspector, click ▼	To hide the Property inspector and expand the document window.
At the bottom of the document window, click ▲	To display the Property inspector. The space available in the document window decreases.

Topic C: Editing pages

Explanation

You'll probably spend most of your time in Dreamweaver editing Web pages and managing Web sites. Editing content in Dreamweaver is a lot like using a word processor. You can add, edit, delete, and re-arrange content (such as text, tables, and images) on a page. You can save a group of Web pages as a site, similar to saving word-processor pages together as a single document.

Pages in a word-processor document are typically designed to be read in sequence—when you finish reading page 6, for example, you continue on to page 7. However, pages in a Web site can be linked in any order, or they can follow no order at all.

Web page elements

Web pages can include many types of content, including text, tables, images, and links, as illustrated in Exhibit 1-5.

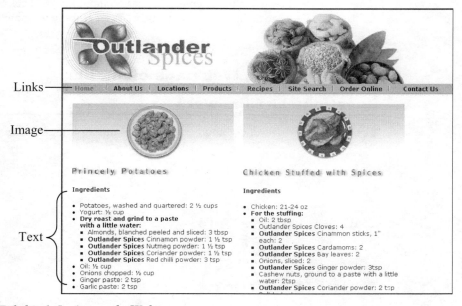

Exhibit 1-5: A sample Web page

The following table describes some typical Web page elements.

Element	Description
Text	Words, phrases, sentences, headings, and paragraphs.
Table	A grid structure consisting of rows and columns meant primarily to contain tabular data, such as a product list with associated prices. Tables can also help you control the layout and spacing of elements on a page.
Image	A graphic file, typically in the .gif, .jpg, or .png format.
Link	Text or an image that connects the browser to another location when clicked. The destination might be another Web page, a different area of the current page, or some other resource.
Image map	A single graphic that can include multiple links. *(click map – See photo)*
Forms	Interactive pages consisting of text input fields, check boxes, and buttons that allow the user to submit data to a server for processing and data storage.

Do it!

C-1: Discussing Web page elements

Questions and answers

1 What's the difference between an image and an image map?

2 What are links?

3 What is a table used for?

4 What are forms?

Text basics

Explanation

To add text to a Web page, you can simply type at the insertion point, just as you would in a word-processing program. You can also add text by copying it or dragging it from another application or Web page. After you enter text, you can format it.

Inserting and editing text can sometimes change the position of the text on the page, or it might cause other elements on the page to move. For example, an image that follows a paragraph might move down as more text is added to a paragraph, thus increasing the vertical length of the paragraph.

Do it!

C-2:   Inserting and editing text

Here's how	Here's why
1 Click the green text box near the top of the page	To select it. You'll modify the text in this section.
2 Click to the left of **spices**, as shown	rich heritage of spices from all You can find our kiosks in grocer To place the insertion point at this location.
3 Type **the finest**	To add text to the paragraph.
Press (SPACEBAR)	rich heritage of the finest spices 1e world. You can find our kiosks To add a space. This type of text editing is no different from working in a word processor.
4 Place the insertion point as shown	**Featured Products**| Since 600 B.C. Only one product is currently featured, so you'll delete the "s" in "Products."
Press (← BACKSPACE)	To delete the letter.
5 Choose **File**, **Save**	To save index.html.

Basic text formatting

Explanation

When you add text to a page, the text appears in the browser's default font. You can format text to suit an overall design scheme and improve the readability of the text. You can change the formatting of text by using the Text menu.

Applying a font set

Dreamweaver provides some default font sets that you can apply to text. You can also create your own font sets. You can use the Type menu to apply a font set or change the font size and style.

To apply a font set:

1 Select the text that you want to format.

2 Choose Text, Font, and then select a font set.

Do it!

C-3: Formatting text

Here's how	Here's why
1 Select the indicated text	We bring you a rich heritage of the finest spices from all over the world. You can find our kiosks in grocery and specialty stores all over the country, or you can order directly from this Web site. We are dedicated to providing spices of exceptional quality and variety. Discover a whole new world of flavor: look for an Outlander Spices kiosk in a store near you!
	(Drag the pointer from the beginning to the end of the first paragraph.) You'll apply a font set to this text.
Choose **Text**, **Font**, **Verdana**, **Arial**, **Helvetica**, **sans-serif**	To apply the Verdana font set to the selected text. The last font in a set is a generic typeface: either serif, sans-serif, or monospace. This ensures that at the very least, the type of font you want will be applied no matter what fonts are available on the user's system.
2 Select the remaining text	We bring you a rich heritage of the finest spices from all over the world. You can find our kiosks in grocery and specialty stores all over the country, or you can order directly from this Web site. We are dedicated to providing spices of exceptional quality and variety. Discover a whole new world of flavor: look for an Outlander Spices kiosk in a store near you!
	You'll apply a font set to this text by using another method.
In the Property inspector, click the Font list and choose **Verdana**, **Arial**, **Helvetica**, **sans-serif**	To apply the Verdana font set to the selected text.

3 Click the text box below
   In the News

   You'll italicize this text.

   Select the first sentence in the first paragraph

   Choose **Text**, **Style**, **Emphasis**

   To apply the italic style to the selected text. Emphasis means that the <em> tag is used. Different browsers might format the emphasized text differently, but most browsers render it in italics.

4 Select the first sentence in the next paragraph

   You'll apply emphasis by using another method.

   In the Property inspector, click *I*

   To apply the italic style to the selected text. In most cases, browsers will apply the same italic formatting to text with the emphasis style applied to it.

5 Save index.html

   Choose File, Save or click the Save button.

Adding images

Explanation

Web designers often use images to convey or reinforce ideas in ways that text alone cannot. A Web page that includes images is typically more visually appealing and inviting to the user than is a page with just text.

When you add an image, Dreamweaver prompts you to enter an alternate text string for the image. (A text "string" is developer parlance for a word, phrase, or sentence.) If you point to an image that has alternate text provided, some browsers will show the text as a tooltip. Alternate text should describe either the content or the purpose of the image—whichever is most appropriate. Users that have images disabled in their browsers or who use non-visual browsers will be able to read the alternate text and understand its context in the document.

To insert an image in a Web page:

1 In the Files panel, navigate to the folder containing the images for the current site.
2 Drag the image file to the document window.
3 In the Image Tag Accessibility Attributes dialog box, type alternate text if desired, and click OK.

You can then adjust the size and position of an image by using the options in the Property inspector.

Internet Graphic .JPG should be @ 72 dpi for Web Images.

Do it!

C-4: Adding an image

Here's how	Here's why
1 In the Files panel, navigate to the images folder	(In the outlanderspices.com folder, which is in the current unit folder.) You'll insert an image on the current page.
2 Drag **home_image.jpg** to the document window, as shown	
	To place the image on the page. The Image Tag Accessibility Attributes dialog box appears.
3 In the Alternate text box, type **The Market leader in quality spices**	To assign an alternate text string to this image.
4 Click **OK**	To close the Image Tag Accessibility Attributes dialog box.
5 Save index.html	

mozilla Firefox

Previewing Web pages

Explanation

You can preview a Web page while you're working on it so that you can see how it will appear in a particular Web browser.

Using multiple browsers

Not all browsers render a Web page the same way—there are often minor differences in how each browser interprets HTML code, and these can affect the way a page looks and functions. For this reason, it's a good idea to preview your Web pages in several browsers.

When Dreamweaver is installed, it detects the default browser defined for your computer, and uses that as the primary browser for previewing pages. But you can add up to 20 browsers to the preview menu. Here's how:

1. Choose Edit, Preferences to open the Preferences dialog box.
2. In the Category box, select Preview in Browser.
3. Click the plus sign next to Browsers to open the Add Browser dialog box.
4. In the Name box, type a name for the browser.
5. Click the Browse button, and navigate to the .exe file for the desired browser (typically located in a folder in the C:\Program Files folder).
6. Check Secondary browser.
7. Click OK to close the Add Browser dialog box.
8. Repeat steps 3–7 for each browser you want to add to the preview menu.
9. Click OK to close the Preferences dialog box.

Previewing a Web page

To preview a Web page in a browser:

1. In the Document toolbar, click the "Preview/Debug in browser" button. From the drop-down list that appears, select a browser. The Macromedia Dreamweaver 8 dialog box appears.
2. Click No to preview the page in its saved state. Click Yes to save the page first and then preview it.

Exhibit 1-6: A sample page preview in Internet Explorer

Do it!

C-5: Previewing a page in a browser

Here's how	Here's why
1 In the third paragraph below "In the News," italicize the text **Announcing classes**	(Select the text and click the Italic button in the Property inspector.) You'll make changes and preview them in a browser.
2 Click [icon]	(The "Preview/Debug in browser" button is on the Document toolbar.) A drop-down list appears.
Select **Preview in iexplore**	To view the page in Internet Explorer. The Macromedia Dreamweaver 8 dialog box appears.
Click **Yes**	To save the page in its current state. The page appears in the default browser.
3 Verify that "Announcing classes" is italic	
4 In Dreamweaver, select **Announcing classes** again	You'll change the text back to the way it was, and preview the results in the browser.
Click [*I*]	To remove the italics.
Save your changes	
5 In your browser, refresh the page	To preview the saved changes. The text is no longer italic.
6 Close the browser	

HTML TAG
Body
TITLe

Topic D: HTML basics

Explanation

As you learned earlier, HTML code encloses your text content and defines the basic structure of a Web page. Even if you prefer to work in Design view in Dreamweaver, you'll need to be familiar with basic HTML syntax.

Standard tags

Structure is defined through tags. A *tag* is a command that tells the Web browser how to interpret or display the content enclosed by the tag. For example, the `<h1>` tag identifies a line of text as a level-one heading, and the browser renders it accordingly.

HTML tags are enclosed in angle brackets: `< >`. Most HTML tags consist of a beginning tag and an ending tag. The ending tag includes a forward slash (/), which tells the browser that the tag instruction has ended. For example, the following code is a snippet of text that uses the `<b>` tag to define bold text:

```
Outlander Spices makes the <b>best</b> seasonings.
```

A Web browser would display this text as follows:

Outlander Spices makes the **best** seasonings.

The following code shows the basic structure of an HTML document. Notice that some tags are nested inside other tags, and there is an ending tag for each starting tag.

```
<html>
  <head>
    <title>Document Title</title>
  </head>
  <body>
    All rendered HTML and content is inserted here.
  </body>
</html>
```

The standard tags that begin every HTML document are `<html>`, `<head>`, and `<body>`. The `<html>` element is considered the *root element,* or top-level element. All other HTML tags reside within the `<html>` tag. It defines the document as an HTML document. Every HTML document is then divided into two sections: the `<head>` section and the `<body>` section.

The `<head>` section contains the `<title>` element, which defines the document's title. This section also contains style sheet information, meta information, scripts, and other code or resources that are not rendered on the page.

The `<body>` section contains all the content (text, images, and so on) that is rendered on a page, along with the code for it. If you can see it in a browser, the code for it is in the body section.

Do it!

D-1: Viewing HTML

Here's how	Here's why
1 On the Document toolbar, click ⬒ Split	To split the document window into Code view and Design view.
2 In Design view, click an image on the page	(To select it.) Code view automatically scrolls to the area of the code that defines the selected object. Dreamweaver highlights the code for the selected object.
3 Click <> Code	To switch to Code view.
4 Locate the `<html>` tag What's the purpose of this element?	Near the top of the page.
5 Locate the `<head>` tag What's the purpose of this element?	→ CONTAINS TITLE TAG MBTA DATA ETC... plus Description And Key woords
6 Locate the `<body>` tag What's the purpose of this element?	
7 Click 🔲 Design	To return to Design view.
8 Close index.html Close Dreamweaver	

Unit summary: Getting started

Topic A   In this topic, you learned a few basics about the Internet, the World Wide Web, and HTML. You learned that HTML is a standard **markup language** used to build Web pages.

Topic B   In this topic, you identified the main components of the **Dreamweaver 8 interface**, including panel groups and the Property inspector.

Topic C   In this topic, you learned how to do **basic editing**, including inserting and formatting text and inserting images. You also learned how to **apply basic font styles** and how to **preview** a Web page in a browser.

Topic D   In this topic, you learned more about **HTML tags**, including basic HTML syntax and the fundamental tags that define the structure of a Web page.

Independent practice activity

In this activity, you'll start Dreamweaver and create a Web page based on an existing page. Then you'll add and format text, and preview the page in a browser. Then you'll change the text formatting and observe the change.

1 Start Dreamweaver 8.

2 From the current unit folder, open the Practice folder.

3 From the Practice folder, open the outlanderspices.com folder.

4 Open index.html, and save it as **homepage.html** in the same folder. Update the link for the logo.jpg image, if necessary.

5 View the source code. (Use either Code view or Split view.)

6 Return to Design view.

7 Add some text of your choice to the document.

8 Format the new text with a font set of your choice.

9 Save homepage.html.

10 Preview the page in the default browser.

11 In the document window, make the text you added bold.

12 Save homepage.html.

13 Refresh the browser.

14 Close the browser.

15 Save and close homepage.html. (Leave Dreamweaver 8 open.)

Review questions

1 The Property inspector is *context sensitive*. What does this mean?

2 In most Web sites, the pages are meant to be read in a particular sequence. True or false?

3 Why are fonts best specified in *font sets*?

4 The text you are reading right now is an example of:

A A serif font

B A sans-serif font

C A monospaced font

D Plain text

5 What are the three most fundamental HTML tags that should be used in every Web page?

A `<title>, <head>, <body>`

B `<html>, <head>, <body>` ✓

C `<start>, <body>, <end>`

D `<html>, <head>, <content>`

Unit 2

Web sites and pages

Unit time: 30 minutes

Complete this unit, and you'll know how to:

A Plan and define a Web site, and use Map view and the Assets panel.

B Create a Web page, import text from external files, and set page properties.

Topic A: Creating a Web site

Explanation

Organizing site files in a logical structure is critical to the successful operation of your Web site. The structure of a Web site affects a developer's ability to maintain the site over time.

Planning

When you start creating a Web site, you might be inclined to first write the content for the pages. But it's best to plan your Web site carefully before you get into the nuts and bolts. Think about how best to structure your pages and content, how you want to present information, and how you want the site to look (color schemes, fonts, and so on) before you begin working on individual pages. Spend some time defining the audience for the site and the goals you want to accomplish with it.

Effective design also results in easier maintenance. Content requirements, design changes, and job assignments typically change over time. You should plan and design a site that will be easy for another developer or team of developers to take over.

Site structure

A well-designed site must have an effective navigation scheme. You need to plan the link relationships between the pages in your site, and organize the site assets into a logical folder structure. Exhibit 2-1 shows a typical folder structure for a Web site. All images are stored in their own folder, and styles, scripts, and multimedia files are also stored separately in logically named folders.

Exhibit 2-1: Typical folder structure for a Web site

Local vs. remote sites

You can set up your site on a local folder (one that's located on your computer's hard drive). This will allow you to test the site before you publish it on the Web. After you test a site locally and verify that it looks and functions as you intended, you can publish it to a remote folder on the Web server that will be hosting your site.

A *local site* serves as the root directory for your Web site. When defining the site's root folder, do not use the root of your hard drive or the Dreamweaver application folder.

To define a local site:

1 Choose Site, New Site.

2 Enter a name for your site.

3 Enter the URL for your site.

4 Click Next, and complete the screens for the Site Definition Wizard. The last screen displays a summary.

5 Click Done to create the site.

Do it!

A-1: Defining a site

Here's how	Here's why
1 Choose **Site**, **New Site...**	The Site Definition Wizard appears. You'll create a Web site.
2 For the site name, enter **outlanderspices.com** For the HTTP address, enter **http://outlanderspices.com** Click **Next**	
3 Verify that "No, I do not want to use a server technology" is selected Click **Next**	The Editing Files, Part 3 screen appears.
4 Verify that "Edit local copies on my machine" is selected Click 🗀	To open the "Choose local root folder for outlanderspices.com" dialog box.
5 Browse to the outlanderspices.com folder	In the current unit folder.
Open the folder and click **Select**	To specify where the files for this site should be stored.
Click **Next**	The Sharing Files screen appears.
6 From the top list, select **None**	You won't connect to a remote server in this course.
Click **Next**	The Summary screen appears.
7 Click **Done**	To create the site.

8 Observe the Files panel

Outlanderspices.com is listed as a Web site.

Map view

Explanation

You can display your Web site in diagram form by using Map view. Map view displays the site pages and the link relationships among them. Map view can help you define the structure and navigation of your site. To switch to Map view, select Map View from the Site view list in the Files panel.

The Assets panel

Dreamweaver keeps track of your site's *assets*, which are the components of your site, such as images or multimedia files. The Assets panel displays a list of images and other assets, and displays information about each file, such as its dimensions, file size, file type, and path.

Do it!

A-2: Using Map view and the Assets panel

Here's how	Here's why
1 From the Site view list, select **Map view**, as shown	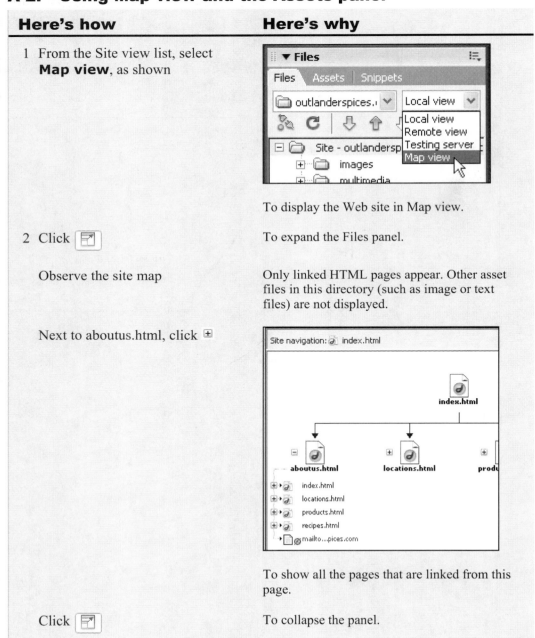
	To display the Web site in Map view.
2 Click ⬚	To expand the Files panel.
Observe the site map	Only linked HTML pages appear. Other asset files in this directory (such as image or text files) are not displayed.
Next to aboutus.html, click ⊞	
	To show all the pages that are linked from this page.
Click ⬚	To collapse the panel.

3 Return to Local view   From the Site view list, select Local view.

   Press (F5)   To refresh the view of the panel.

   Detach the Files panel group   (Drag from the panel group's gripper to the
                                           center of the screen.) The Files panel group
                                           appears in a separate window.

4 Activate the Assets panel   You'll view the image files used in this site.

   Click 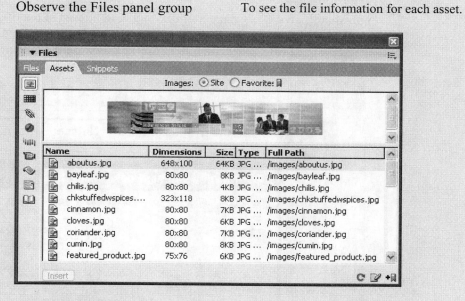   (If necessary.) To see the image files.

   Expand the Files panel group   Move the pointer over the bottom-right corner of
                                           the window until the pointer changes to a
                                           double-sided arrow; then drag.

   Observe the Files panel group   To see the file information for each asset.

5 Activate the Files panel

6 Drag the Files panel group back to
   the other panel groups

Topic B: Creating Web pages

Explanation

Dreamweaver makes it easy to add Web pages to a site. You can also add text and change the color of the text and the page background.

Creating a basic page

To create a Web page:

1   Choose File, New to open the New Document dialog box.
2   From the Category list, select Basic page.
3   From the Basic page list, select HTML.
4   Click Create.

Page titles

You should give every page a title, which will appear in the title bar of the browser window. Exhibit 2-1 shows the title of a page viewed in three different browsers. To specify a page title, enter the title in the Title box on the Document toolbar.

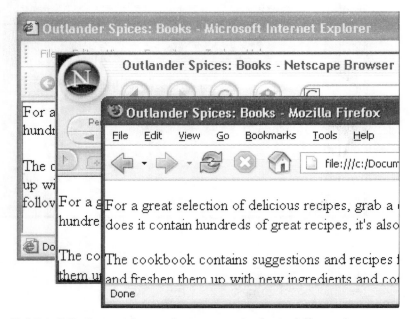

Exhibit 2-2: Page titles as they appear in three different browsers

Do it!

B-1: Creating and titling Web pages

Here's how	Here's why
1 Choose **File**, **New...**	To start creating a Web page. The New Document dialog box appears.
In the Category list, select **Basic page**	If necessary.
In the Basic page list, select **HTML**	If necessary.
Click **Create**	To open a blank HTML page in the document window.
2 On the Document toolbar, edit the Title box to read **Outlander Spices: Books**	Title: `Outlander Spices: Books`
	To give this page a title. This text will appear in the browser window's title bar.
3 Choose **File**, **Save**	The Save As dialog box appears because this is a new document that hasn't been saved yet.
4 Navigate to the outlanderspices.com folder	(If necessary.) In the current unit folder.
Edit the File name box to read **books.html**	File name: `books.html`
Click **Save**	

Inserting and importing text

Explanation

You can add text to a Web page by simply typing in the document window. If the text you need is in a separate file of one sort or another, you can copy and paste the text into Dreamweaver.

It's often helpful to use an external file as the source of your Web site text, so you can distribute the file for editing and approval by other members of a development team. When the text is approved and ready, you can copy and paste it into a Web page. You can use Dreamweaver to import text from a text file or from a formatted document such as a Microsoft Word file.

Importing text files

When you import a text file into a Web page, the Insert Document dialog box appears. It prompts you to specify import and formatting options, as shown in Exhibit 2-3.

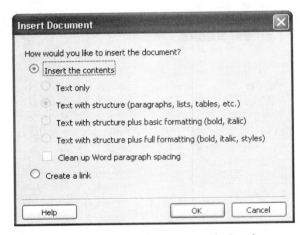

Exhibit 2-3: The Insert Document dialog box

The options in the Insert Document dialog box are described in the following table.

Option	Description
Insert the contents; Create a link	Select one of these two options to define how the text file will be imported. If you insert the contents, the text is copied to the page. If you create a link, a hyperlink to the text file is inserted.
	If you select Insert the contents, the options described next are available.
Text only	Inserts plain text without formatting.
Text with structure	Inserts plain text and retains structures such as paragraph breaks, lists, and tables.
Text with structure plus basic formatting	Inserts plain or structured text. If any text uses basic formatting such as italics or boldface, Dreamweaver retains this formatting by creating basic HTML tags where necessary.
Text with structure plus full formatting	Inserts plain or structured text and retains basic formatting. If any text has a style applied to it, it's added to the Web page in an internal CSS style sheet.

Option	Description
Clean up Word paragraph spacing	Removes extra spacing above and below paragraphs in documents imported from Microsoft Word. Available when "Text with structure" is selected.

Do it!

B-2:   Importing text

Here's how	Here's why
1 From the Files panel, drag **booksinfo1.doc** to the document window	The Insert Document dialog box appears. You'll import text from a Microsoft Word file and from a standard text file.
2 Verify that "Insert the contents" is selected	To directly insert the contents of the Word file onto the Web page.
Verify that "Text with structure plus basic formatting" is selected	To import both the text and its basic formatting.
Check **Clean up Word paragraph spacing**	(If necessary.) To remove unnecessary spaces, carriage returns, and other characters from the text.
Click **OK**	To insert the text as specified. Notice that "Outlander Cooking!" appears in italics.
3 Switch to Code view	Click the Code view button on the Document toolbar.
Observe the text	Dreamweaver applied <em> tags to the italic text to carry the formatting over to the Web page.
Return to Design view	
4 Place the insertion point as shown	new ingredients and combinati easy-to-follow instructions.	
Press ↵ ENTER	To begin a new paragraph after the existing paragraph.
5 Drag **booksinfo2.txt** below the current text	(From the Files panel.) To add more text from another type of file. The Insert Document dialog box appears.
6 Click **OK**	To insert the text and close the Insert Document dialog box. This is a plain text file, so there is no formatting information in it.
7 Save books.html	

Page properties

Explanation

You can change Dreamweaver's default page properties to customize the appearance of a Web page.

Page margins

Different browsers apply their own default Web page margins. A *margin* is the space between a page's content and the browser window. (Margins may also exist between individual elements.) Most browsers apply between 10 and 15 pixels of space to establish a default margin. If you don't specify page margins, then they will be determined by a particular browser's default setting. To ensure that your Web pages appear consistently, it's important that you set a page margin for all your pages. You can even set your page margins to zero so that some of your content, such as a navigation bar or header logo, can appear flush with the edge of the browser window. You can then apply margins to large content sections or individual elements to ensure that other content is offset from the browser window and other page elements.

Background color

By default, Web pages have a white background, but you can change it to any background color you wish. To apply a background color, select a color from the Background color box in the Page Properties dialog box. The Background color box displays a *color picker*—a palette with a set of color swatches, as shown in Exhibit 2-4. By default, the color picker displays the Web Safe Colors, a standard set of 216 colors supported consistently by the vast majority of computers.

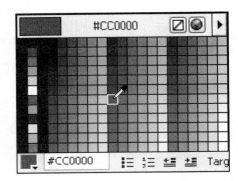

Exhibit 2-4: The color picker displays color swatches

Screen Res Std is 800 x 600

Do it!

B-3: Setting page properties

Here's how	Here's why
1 Choose **Modify, Page Properties...**	To open the Page Properties dialog box. You'll use this to change the appearance of the page.
2 Click the Background color box	A color picker appears. The pointer changes to an eyedropper.
Click as shown	
	In the bottom-right corner.
3 In the Left margin box, enter **0**	To give the page a left margin of zero pixels.
4 In the three other margin boxes, enter **0**	To set the margin to zero on all four sides of the page.
5 Click **OK**	To apply the changes and close the Page Properties dialog box.
6 Save books.html	

Text color

Explanation

By default, all text is black. You can change the color of selected text on a page, or you can set a default color for all text on a page.

To set the default color for all text on the page:

1 Choose Modify, Page Properties to open the Page Properties dialog box.
2 In the Category list, select Appearance.
3 Click the Text color box.
4 Select a color swatch.
5 Click OK.

To change the color of selected text:

1 Select the text.
2 In the Property inspector, click the color picker.
3 Select a color.

Do it!

B-4: Setting text color

Here's how	Here's why
1 In the first paragraph, select **great**	For a great selection o it contain hundreds of You'll change the color of this word.
2 In the Property inspector, click the color picker	
Select a light green color	#33FF00 To apply this color to the selected text.
3 Click the page	To deselect the text. The green text on the yellow background is difficult to read.
4 Apply a darker color to **great**	Select the text. Then, in the Property inspector, click the color picker and select a dark color.
5 Save and close books.html	

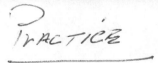
Practice

Unit summary: Web sites and pages

Topic A   In this topic, you learned some basic concepts for **planning** a Web site. You learned how to **define** a Web site, and you used the Files panel to display a site in **Map view**. Finally, you used the Assets panel to view your **site assets**.

Topic B   In this topic, you learned how to create and title **Web pages**. Then you learned how to **import text** from external documents and set **page margins**. Finally, you learned how to apply **color** to a page background and to text.

Independent practice activity

In this activity, you'll define a new Web site, create a Web page, and add text to it. Then you'll set page margins.

1 Choose **Site**, **New Site** to start the Site Definition Wizard.

2 Enter **Outlander** as the site name.

3 Click **Next** and then click **Next** again.

4 On the Editing Files, Part 3 page, navigate to the outlanderspices.com folder. (The outlanderspices.com folder is located in the Practice folder, in the current unit folder.)

5 On the Sharing files page, choose **None** as the server connection, and click **Next**.

6 Click **Done**.

7 Observe the new site in Map view.

8 Create a Web page and title it **Outlander Spices: Videos**.

9 Save the page as **videos.html** in the outlanderspices.com folder, in the Practice folder.

10 Import text from videosinfo.doc into videos.html. (*Hint*: Drag the Microsoft Word file from the Files panel group to the document window. Insert the text with structure plus basic formatting.)

11 Set all four page margins to **20**. (*Hint*: Choose **Modify**, **Page Properties**.)

12 Give the page a light background color of your choice.

13 Set a new default text color of your choice.

14 Make the text **spice up your recipes** appear in a different color than the rest of the text.

15 Save and close videos.html.

Review questions

1 Page titles appear as headings on a page. True or false?

2 Before you start creating a Web site, you should always:
MAP IT OUT, CONTENT FUNCTIONALITY, FLASH, MULTIMEDIA ETC.

3 Why is it often a good idea to set your own page margins?

4 Why is it important to select text and background colors carefully?

5 Name three important factors that you should consider when planning a Web site.

Unit 3
Text formatting

Unit time: 60 minutes

Complete this unit, and you'll know how to:

A Create paragraphs and insert special characters.

B Create a page structure, and apply HTML styles and list formats.

C Create CSS style sheets, and apply styles to text.

Topic A: Text basics

Explanation

When you type text in Dreamweaver, it appears on the page, starting at the insertion point. However, some characters cannot be entered into an HTML document by typing them. These special characters must be entered as HTML codes instead.

Line breaks and paragraph breaks

In a word processor, you use line breaks and paragraph breaks to mark the end of lines and paragraphs. A line break forces text to begin on a new line, but within the same paragraph. A paragraph break begins a new line and marks the end of a paragraph. These codes are usually hidden in a word-processing document, but they can be displayed if necessary, as shown in Exhibit 3-1. Dreamweaver uses its own visual cues to indicate line breaks and paragraph breaks.

```
This·sentence·ends·in·a·line·break. ↵
This·second·sentence·ends·in·a·line·break. ↵
All·three·lines·are·part·of·the·same·paragraph. ¶
```

```
This·sentence·ends·in·a·paragraph·break. ¶
This·second·sentence·is·a·separate·paragraph. ¶
```

Exhibit 3-1: Line breaks (top) and paragraph breaks (bottom) in a word-processing document

Line and paragraph breaks in Dreamweaver

Many of Dreamweaver's text formatting tools and shortcuts are paragraph-based, which means that text formatting is applied to an entire paragraph. If you copy text from a word processor into a Web page in Dreamweaver, line breaks and paragraph breaks are converted automatically to HTML tags. To apply formatting to individual paragraphs, you must define them as separate paragraphs.

If you need to convert multiple instances of a code, such as a line break, to another code, such as a paragraph break, you can use the Find and Replace window to change each instance. This can help you save time and prevent omissions.

Do it!   **A-1:   Changing line breaks to paragraph breaks**

Here's how	Here's why
1 In the Files panel, browse to the outlanderspices.com folder	(In the current unit folder.) You'll separate headings from text with paragraph breaks so you can apply paragraph formatting.
Open aboutus.html	
2 Choose **Edit**, **Preferences...**	To open the Preferences dialog box. You'll show line breaks to make it easier to work with the text.
In the Category list, select **Invisible Elements**	
Check **Line breaks**	[BR] ☑ Line breaks
Click **OK**	To close the Preferences dialog box and display line breaks in the document window.
3 Locate the text "All Spiced Up"	All Spiced Up [BR] Outlander Spices oper world and select gourn
	(In Design view.) This text is on a separate line but is still part of the paragraph that follows it. If you want the heading and the text that follows it to have different styles, you need to make them separate paragraphs.
4 Select **All Spiced Up**, as shown	All Spiced Up [BR] Outlander Spices ope world and select gour
5 Click [Split]	To split the document window into Code view and Design view. The selection in Design view is also highlighted in Code view.
In Code view, observe the HTML tags at the beginning and end of the heading	`<p>`All Spiced Up` ` Outlander Spices opened
	The line begins with a paragraph tag and ends with a line-break tag. The `<p>` tag indicates the start of a paragraph, and the ` ` tag is the line break.

6 In Design view, click the line-break icon as shown

All Spiced Up
Outlander Spices ope

To select it. You'll replace this line break with a paragraph break.

Press (DELETE)

In Design view, the line-break icon is deleted. In Code view, the `<br>` tag is deleted.

Press (↵ ENTER)

To replace the line break with a paragraph break.

7 Observe Code view

```
<p>All Spiced Up</p>
<p>Outlander Spices open
t quality spices from all
```

A closing paragraph tag now marks the end of the text "All Spiced Up," and an opening paragraph tag now marks the beginning of the next line of text.

8 Observe Design view

All Spiced Up

Outlander Spices op

The line-break icon is gone, and a larger space separates the title and the text below it.

9 Choose **Edit**, **Find and Replace...**

To open the Find and Replace dialog box. You'll replace the remaining line-break tags with paragraph tags.

In the Search list, select **Source Code**

To search in Code view.

In the Find box, enter **\<br\>**

You'll look for all instances of the line-break tag.

In the Replace box, enter **\</p\>\<p\>**

To replace the next instance of `<br>` with `</p>`, the closing paragraph tag, and `<p>`, the starting paragraph tag.

10 Click **Find Next**

To find the next occurrence of the `<br>` tag.

11 Click **Replace**	To replace the tag.
Click in Design view	To force Design view to update. The "About our spices" heading was converted to a separate paragraph.
Click **Replace All**	To replace the remaining line-break tags with paragraph tags. The Results panel group appears below the Property inspector.
12 Observe the Results panel group	The Search tab displays a list of the replacements that were made.
Right-click the Search tab and select **Close panel group**	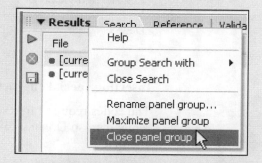
	To close the Results panel group.
13 Save your changes	

Special characters

Explanation

Some characters that you might need in your content are not included on a computer keyboard, such as the copyright symbol (©) or specific language characters, like the umlaut (ü). You can insert these special characters in a Web page by using their corresponding character entities, which are HTML codes that begin with an ampersand (&) and end with a semicolon. The following table lists some common examples.

Character	Symbol	HTML code
Copyright	©	`&copy;`
Registered trademark	®	`&reg;`
Degree	°	`&deg;`

Inserting special characters

The codes required for these special characters are not always intuitive or easy to remember, so Dreamweaver provides a list you can select from. To insert a special character:

1 In Code view, place the insertion point where you want the special character to appear.

2 Type & (ampersand). A list of special characters appears.

3 Scroll through the list to find the desired character. The HTML code for the character appears in the right column in black, and the character appears in the left column in blue.

4 Select a character from the list.

Adding spaces

HTML recognizes only one space character between words. To insert more than one space, you can use the *non-breaking space* character (` `). This HTML code adds a single space without forcing a line break.

Do it!

A-2:   Inserting special characters and spaces

Here's how	Here's why
1 In Code view, scroll to the bottom of the page	You'll replace the word "Copyright" with the copyright symbol.

Select **Copyright**, as shown

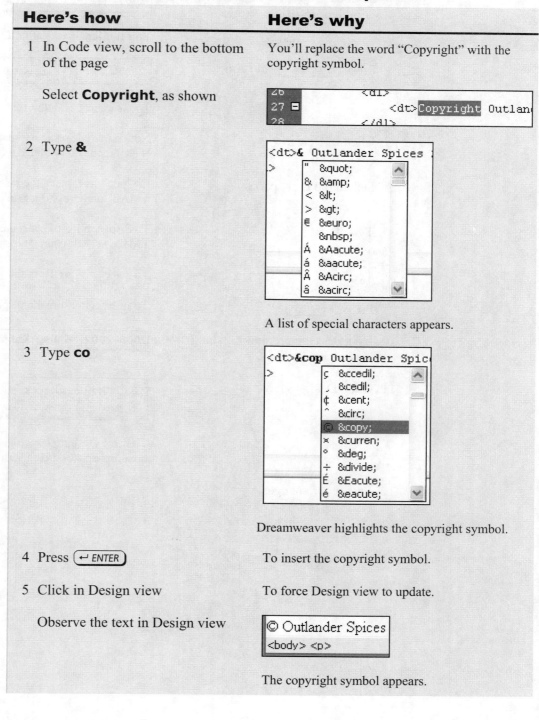

2 Type **&**	

A list of special characters appears.

3 Type **co**	

Dreamweaver highlights the copyright symbol.

4 Press (↵ ENTER)	To insert the copyright symbol.
5 Click in Design view	To force Design view to update.

Observe the text in Design view

The copyright symbol appears.

6   In Code view, place the insertion point before **All**, as shown

| -2007. |All rights reserved |

You'll insert spaces after the copyright notice.

Press SPACEBAR four times

| -2007. |All rights reserved |

To insert spaces in the HTML code.

7   Click in Design view

Notice that the ordinary spaces entered in the HTML code do not have any effect.

8   Delete the four spaces

In Code view, place the insertion point in front of "All" and press Backspace four times.

9   Type **&**

To display a list of special characters. You'll add the HTML character for a space.

Type **nb**

To select nbsp; from the list.

Press ↵ ENTER

To insert a non-breaking space.

10 Insert three more non-breaking spaces, as shown

| 2005-2007.   All |

11 Click Design view

| © Outlander Spices 2005-2007.   All right |
| <body> <p> |

To force Design view to update. The four non-breaking spaces create additional space.

12 Save your changes

8 NB SP; For multiple spaces

Topic B: Structural formatting

Explanation

Headings, paragraphs, and other structural elements allow you to organize a Web page into a logical hierarchy, which can make your pages more searchable, easier to read, and easier for other developers to modify. A well-designed page structure can also make it easier to design and arrange your page content and make your content accessible to users with alternative browsing devices.

Paragraph formatting

As in a word-processing document, you can align Web-page paragraphs to the left, right, or center, or you can justify them. To do so, click in the paragraph you want to align, and then click the Align Left, Align Right, Align Center, or Justify button in the Property inspector.

To define a line of text as a heading or subheading, click the paragraph and select a heading from the Format list in the Property inspector. Or, you can choose Text, Paragraph Format, and then select a heading.

Document structure

If you want to create a heading for a page or a section, you should define the text as a heading, and not simply change the appearance of the text to *resemble* a heading. The heading level you choose should logically reflect the nature of the content. For example, if you have a heading that serves as the top-level heading on a page, you should define it as Heading 1. To do so, select the text, and in the Property inspector, select Heading 1 from the Format list. In the code, this command will assign the <h1> tag to the text. You can also manually enclose the text in an <h1> tag if you prefer to work with code when you build your document structure.

Using meaningful and logical structures—such as Heading 1 for top-level headings and Heading 2 for subheadings—will help establish consistency on your pages, save you time and effort when you later update your pages, and allow your pages to be indexed by search engines more efficiently. The use of headings can also improve the readability of a page. A page that's neatly structured into sections will help readers find what they're looking for.

Structural tags

When you're creating a Web page, think of it as a traditional outline, and structure it accordingly. HTML provides a set of six headings you can use to structure your documents. The tags for these headings are <h1> through <h6>. They each have their own default formatting. All headings appear bold by default, and they appear in different font sizes. The <h1> tag applies the largest default font size, and the <h6> applies the smallest default font size. For example, if you're creating a page intended to deliver company news, an effective structure might look something like this:

```
<h1>Company News</h1>
<p>First paragraph of Company News...</p>
<p>Second paragraph of Company News...</p>
<h2>Subheading of Company News</h2>
<p>First paragraph of sub-topic...</p>
```

When you're establishing your document structure, don't focus on how each element appears in the browser—you can change that later. Instead, think about how best to define the content you're working with, creating a logical arrangement of headings, paragraphs, and lists. You can customize the styles for any HTML tag by using CSS.

Do it!

B-1: Applying structural tags

Here's how	Here's why
1 Click inside the copyright text	At the bottom of the page.
In the Property inspector, click ☰	To center the copyright text. You can also choose Text, Align, Center.
2 Click the line with "All Spiced Up"	To place the insertion point in this line. Paragraph formatting always applies to an entire paragraph.
In the Property inspector, from the Format list, select **Heading 1**	To convert the text to a level-one heading. You can also choose Text, Paragraph Format, Heading 1.
3 Switch to Code view	
Observe the heading code	The text is enclosed in `<h1>` tags to define it as a level-one heading.
Return to Design view	
4 Convert "Expansion project" to a level-one heading	Click in the paragraph. Then, in the Property inspector, select Heading 1 from the Format list.
5 Convert the two remaining headings to level-two headings	(The two titles that begin with "About our….") Click each paragraph and select Heading 2 from the Format list in the Property inspector.
6 Save and close aboutus.html	

Lists

Dreamweaver makes it easy to structure content as lists. There are three types of lists you can use: unordered lists, ordered lists, and definition lists. In an unordered list, a bullet, circle, square, or other icon precedes each list item. By default, an unordered list uses bullets, as shown in Exhibit 3-2. Use an unordered list when the sequence of the list items is not important or relevant.

Our most popular spices include:

- Bay leaf
- Cinnamon
- Coriander
- Nutmeg
- Turmeric

Exhibit 3-2: An example of an unordered list

In an ordered list, a number or letter indicates each item's order in the list. By default, ordered lists are numbered 1, 2, 3, and so on. You can also choose Alphabet Large (A, B, C), Alphabet Small (a, b, c), Roman Large (I, II, III), or Roman Small (i, ii, iii). Use an ordered list when the sequence of items is important.

Directions:

1. Whisk the yogurt with the paste. Mix well.
2. Heat the oil, reduce the heat, and then add onions, ginger and garlic.
3. Add the potatoes and fry until golden brown.
4. Add the yogurt paste.
5. Cook for 5 minutes.
6. Add ¾ cup of warm water. Bring to a boil and reduce heat.
7. Cook until the potatoes are tender and the gravy is thick.

Exhibit 3-3: An example of an ordered list

You can also create a definition list, which does not use bullets or numbers. Instead, a definition list is used for terms and their definitions, for use in glossaries, "frequently asked questions" (FAQs) pages, or similar contexts. As shown in Exhibit 3-4, each definition is indented beneath its term. This indentation is the only default formatting that browsers apply to a definition list.

Cinnamon
  Cinnamon is one of our most popular spices, due to its sweet flavor and prominent role in baked goods and candies. Cinnamon is also wonderful in stews and sauces.
Nutmeg
  Nutmeg comes from the seed of a tropical tree. It has a sweet, rich and aromatic flavor that complements meats, vegetables, tomato sauces, and baked goods.

Exhibit 3-4: An example of a definition list

Nested lists

A *nested list* is a list inside another list. For example, a step in a list of instructions might require its own list of sub-steps. Dreamweaver makes it easy to create nested lists. Within the outer list, select the content that you want to turn into a nested list, and click Text Indent in the Property inspector.

Do it!

B-2: Creating lists

Here's how	Here's why
1 Open recipes.html	(From the outlanderspices.com folder in the current unit folder.) You'll convert ordinary text to ordered and unordered lists.
2 In Design view, select all paragraphs between the "Ingredients" and "Directions" subheadings, as shown	Potatoes, washed and quartered: 2 ½ cups Oil: ½ cup Onions chopped: ½ cup Yogurt: ½ cup **Dry roast and grind to a paste with a little water:** Almonds, blanched peeled and sliced: 3 tbsp Outlander Spices Cinnamon powder: 1 ½ tsp Outlander Spices Nutmeg powder: 1 ½ tsp Outlander Spices Coriander powder: 1 ½ tsp Outlander Spices Red chili powder: 3 tsp Garlic paste: 2 tsp Ginger paste: 2 tsp You'll convert these paragraphs to a single unordered list.

3 Choose **Text**, **List**, **Unordered List**

To change the selected text to an unordered list.

Click in Design view

Ingredients

- Potatoes, washed and quartered: 2 ½ cups
- Oil: ½ cup
- Onions chopped: ½ cup
- Yogurt: ½ cup
- **Dry roast and grind to a paste** 📑
  with a little water:
- Almonds, blanched peeled and sliced: 3 tbsp
- Outlander Spices Cinnamon powder: 1 ½ tsp
- Outlander Spices Nutmeg powder: 1 ½ tsp
- Outlander Spices Coriander powder: 1 ½ tsp
- Outlander Spices Red chili powder: 3 tsp
- Garlic paste: 2 tsp
- Ginger paste: 2 tsp

Directions:

To deselect the paragraphs. The paragraphs are converted to items in an unordered list, which is a more appropriate structure for this particular content.

4 Switch to Code view

Click the Show Code view button.

Observe the code for the unordered list

```
15        <ul>
16          <li>Potatoes, washed a
17          <li>Oil: &frac12; cup<
18          <li>Onions chopped: &f
19          <li>Yogurt: &frac12; c
20          <li><strong>Dry roast
21              with a little
22          <li>Almonds, blanched
23          <li>Outlander Spices C
24          <li>Outlander Spices N
25          <li>Outlander Spices C
26          <li>Outlander Spices R
27          <li>Garlic paste: 2 ts
28          <li>Ginger paste: 2 ts
29        </ul>
```

Each item in the list is defined by the `<li>` tag, and every list item is nested inside the `<ul>` tag, which is the unordered-list tag.

Return to Design view

5 Select the paragraphs under "Directions," as shown

> Whisk the yogurt with the roasted paste. M
>
> Heat the oil: reduce the heat, add onions, gu
>
> Add the potatoes and fry until golden brown
> water. Bring to a boil, reduce heat, and coo
> \<body>

You'll convert these paragraphs to an ordered list.

6 Choose **Text**, **List**, **Ordered List**

To convert the text to an ordered list.

Deselect the text

> Directions:
>
> 1. Whisk the yogurt with the roasted pa
> 2. Heat the oil: reduce the heat, add on
> 3. Add the potatoes and fry until golder
>   warm water. Bring to a boil, reduce
> \<body> \<ul> \<li>

(Click the Layout window.) The text is now an ordered list with three sequential steps.

7 Select all list items from "Almonds" to "Red chili powder," as shown

> • **Dry roast and grind to a paste with a little water:**
> • Almonds, blanched peeled and sl
> • Outlander Spices Cinnamon pow
> • Outlander Spices Nutmeg powde
> • Outlander Spices Coriander pow
> • Outlander Spices Red chili powd
> • Garlic paste: 2 tsp

You'll indent these list items to create a nested list.

8 Choose **Text**, **Indent**

> • **Dry roast and grind to a paste with a little water:**
>   ○ Almonds, blanched peelec
>   ○ Outlander Spices Cinnamo
>   ○ Outlander Spices Nutmeg
>   ○ Outlander Spices Coriand
>   ○ Outlander Spices Red chil
> • Garlic paste: 2 tsp

To indent this part of the list and create a nested list. The items are indented and have a different default bullet style. You can specify different bullet styles if necessary.

9 Choose **Text**, **List**, **Properties**	To open the List Properties dialog box.
From the Style list, select **Square**	To change the bullets for the nested list to squares.
Click **OK**	

- Dry roast and grind to a paste with a little water:
  - Almonds, blanched peeled
  - Outlander Spices Cinnamo
  - Outlander Spices Nutmeg
  - Outlander Spices Coriand
  - Outlander Spices Red chil
- Garlic paste: 2 tsp

To apply the new bullet style to the selected items.

10 Deselect the text

11 Save and close recipes.html

Topic C: Cascading Style Sheets

Explanation

HTML tags define the structure of your Web pages. CSS (Cascading Style Sheets) is the standard style language for the Web, and it allows you to control how HTML elements appear in a browser. For example, you can use CSS to define how `<h1>` elements look on all the pages in your site or on a particular page.

You can change the default styles that browsers apply to certain HTML elements. For example, by default, all browsers make text inside an `<h1>` tag large and bold. You can change the default styles for headings or any other rendered element. You can control elements of page design and layout, such as margins, spacing, colors, and font styles. What makes CSS especially powerful is that you can link multiple pages to a style sheet so that you can change any number of Web pages by simply changing style rules once.

This can save a lot of time when you need to update a site's design, and it ensures a consistent appearance throughout a site. CSS also allows you to create leaner, more efficient pages because the style rules are listed only once in a style sheet, rather than repeated in the code on every page.

Internal and external style sheets

You can define and apply styles for HTML elements by using external or internal style sheets (or both).

- **External style sheet** — You define styles in a text file saved with a .css extension. Then, link your Web pages to the style sheet. Use external style sheets whenever you want the style to be global—when you want the styles to apply to multiple documents in a Web site. When you change a style in an external style sheet, the change is reflected in every page linked to that style sheet.
- **Internal style sheet** — You define styles in the `<head>` section of an individual Web page. Internal styles apply only to the page in which they defined. This is useful when you want to make some exceptions to the site's style rules and specify something different for just that page.

You can mix internal and external style sheets in a Web page or site.

Defining styles

The most common types of CSS styles are described in the following table.

Style type	Description

Element styles	These define the formatting of HTML elements. An element style overrides the default formatting for that HTML element. The syntax to define an element style is:
	
	`element { property: value; }`
	
	For example, if you wanted elements using the paragraph tag to be in bold type, you would write the rule this way:
	
	`p { font-weight: bold; }`

Style type	Description

Class styles	Classes enable you to give names to your HTML elements. This allows you to define elements and page sections specifically, rather than relying on the default HTML tag names. For example, you can create a class of the <p> element named "important" that applies bold, red text. Any paragraphs that are given that class name will appear with those formats. You can apply class styles to multiple elements on a page. The syntax for a class style is:
	
	`.className { property: value; }`
	
	The class name must begin with a period. For example, if you wanted to create the rule mentioned above, you would write:
	
	`.important { font-weight: bold; color: red; }`

ID styles	ID styles also allow you to create and name your own elements. However, while a class style can be applied to multiple elements in a page, an ID style can be applied to only one element per page. ID styles are particularly useful for defining major content sections that appear only once on a page, such as a <div> element named "navigation" to define a navigation bar, or a <div> element named "footer" to define the page footer. The syntax for an ID style is:
	
	`#IDname { property: value; }`
	
	The ID name must begin with the number sign (#). For example:
	
	`#footer { font-size: 10px; color: gray; }`

After you create class or ID styles, you need to apply them to the desired HTML elements. When you do so, Dreamweaver applies the class or id attribute directly to that HTML tag. For example, if you apply the class and ID styles mentioned previously to a paragraph and a div element, the HTML will look like this:

```
<p class="important">Paragraph text</p>

<div id="footer">Page footer text</div>
```

You don't need to learn the details of CSS coding to start applying CSS styles to your Web pages. You can create the styles by using panel groups, dialog boxes, and other methods, and Dreamweaver will write the necessary code for you.

C-1:   Discussing style sheets

Questions and answers

1   What's a style sheet?

2   What are the two main types of style sheets?

3   What are the advantages of using an external style sheet?

4   When might you want to use an internal style sheet?

5   What is CSS?

6   Name three types of styles you can define in a style sheet.

7   If you want all level-one headings in your site to appear in gray text, what type of style should you use?

8   Describe a scenario in which you would want to create a class style.

9   Describe a scenario in which you would want to create an ID style.

External style sheets

Explanation   Dreamweaver makes it easy to create external style sheets and attach Web pages to them. To create an external style sheet:

1 Choose File, New to open the New Document dialog box.

2 Under Category, select Basic page, and then select CSS. This will create a blank style-sheet file. (You an also select the CSS Style Sheets category and select a prebuilt CSS style sheet from the list.)

3 Click Create.

4 Save the file and name it with a .css extension. (You should first create a folder named "styles" inside your Web site's folder. Save the style sheet in the styles folder.)

To link a Web page to an external style sheet:

1 Open the Web page.

2 In the CSS Styles panel, click the Attach Style Sheet button to open the Attach External Style Sheet dialog box.

3 Click Browse to open the Select Style Sheet File dialog box.

4 Navigate to the desired .css file.

5 Click OK to select the file and close the Select Style Sheet File dialog box.

6 Click OK to attach this file and close the Attach External Style Sheet dialog box.

Do it!

C-2: Creating and attaching an external style sheet

Here's how	Here's why
1 Choose **File**, **New...**	To open the New Document dialog box.
In the Category list, select **CSS Style Sheets**	
In the CSS Style Sheets list, click **Basic: Verdana**	To select a basic style sheet that sets three commonly used tags in the Verdana font.
2 Click **Create**	To create the CSS file. The style sheet opens in the document window. This style sheet has three rules: one for the body element; one for the table-data tag (table cells); and another for the table-header tag. These styles are all the same because some browsers do not allow text in tables to inherit styles from the body element.
Save the style sheet as **globalstyles.css** in the styles folder	The styles folder is inside the outlanderspices.com folder, in the current unit folder.
Close globalstyles.css	
3 Open aboutus.html	You'll attach the style sheet to this page. The text appears with default styles.
4 Activate the CSS panel group	
Click ⊞	(The Attach Style Sheet button.) The Attach External Style Sheet dialog box appears.
5 Click **Browse**	The Select Style Sheet File dialog box appears.
Navigate to the styles folder	In the outlanderspices.com folder, in the current unit folder.
6 Select **globalstyles.css**	
Click **OK**	To attach the style sheet to this page and close the Select Style Sheet File dialog box.
Confirm that Link is selected	To create a link to this style sheet, rather than embedding its styles directly in aboutus.html.
Click **OK**	To close the Attach External Style Sheet dialog box.
7 Observe the text in aboutus.html	The text now appears in the Verdana font.

8 Switch to Code view

(Click the Show Code view button at the top of the document window.) You'll view the link code.

Locate the link to the style sheet

```
9            <link href="styles/globalstyles.css"
```

(Around line 9.) The code now includes a link to globalstyles.css.

Return to Design view

9 Save aboutus.html

Styles for text

Explanation

There are many styles that you can apply to text, including the font size, font weight (degree of boldness), font style (italics and underlining), and font (typeface).

Font-size units

There are several units of measurement you can use to control font size. The most commonly used are points and pixels. A point is a unit of print measurement that does not translate well to the screen. Pixels are a more appropriate choice for display on a Web page. Using pixels typically produces the most consistent results across different browsers and platforms.

Font sets

One way you can format text is to apply a font set. A *font set* contains a list of similar fonts. When you apply a font set, the Web browser tries to use the first font specified in the set. If the first font is not available on the viewer's system, the browser looks for the second font in the set. If that font is not available, the browser tries to apply the third font in the set, and so on. A font set should end with a generic font specification: either serif, sans-serif, or monospaced.

As demonstrated in Exhibit 3-5, a serif font has *flourishes* (decorations) at the ends of its characters, and sans-serif fonts do not. For example, the text in this paragraph is set in a serif font (Times New Roman). The topic titles and activity titles in this book are set in a sans-serif font (Arial Black). In a monospaced font, every character uses the same amount of space; for example, an "i" and an "m" take up the same amount of space on a line. Monospaced fonts (such as Courier and Courier New) resemble typewriter text. The code examples in this book are set in Courier New.

Dreamweaver provides predefined font sets you can use to help ensure that a wide audience will see your text the way you intend it to be seen.

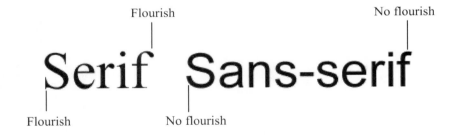

Exhibit 3-5: Serif and sans-serif fonts

Creating and applying element styles

To create an element style:

1 Open one of the following:
   - A Web page (to define a style that applies to only that page)
   - A style sheet (to define a style in the external style sheet)
2 In the CSS Styles panel, click the New CSS Rule button.
3 In the New CSS Rule dialog box, under Selector type, select Tag.
4 In the Tag list, select the HTML tag (element) that you'll be applying the style to.
5 Under Define in, do one of the following:
   - In the list, select a new or existing style sheet file.
   - Select This document only (to create the style in the active document).
6 Click OK.
7 In the CSS Rule Definition dialog box, set the attributes for the style.
8 Click OK.

Do it!

C-3: Defining element styles

Here's how	Here's why
1 In the CSS Styles panel, click [All]	(If necessary.) To display the style sheet files. You will define styles for the `<body>` element and create heading styles.
Double-click **globalstyles.css**	To open the style sheet. There are three styles: body, td, and th. The td rule sets styles for text inside regular table cells, and the th rule sets styles for all table-heading cells.
Activate aboutus.html	(Click the tab at the top of the document window.) The changes you make in the CSS file will apply to elements on this page.
2 In the style tree, click **body**	
	You'll define the styles for the body element. This will set the default page styles for all pages linked to this style sheet, because all elements are inside the body section and therefore inherit its styles.
Click [🖉]	(The Edit Style button.) To edit the body style. The CSS Rule Definition dialog box appears.
From the Size list, select **12**, as shown	Size: [12 ▼] [pixels ▼]
	To set the size of the body text to 12 pixels. The default unit of measurement is pixels.
Click **OK**	The body text in aboutus.html changes in accordance with the style rule.
3 Click [⊡]	(The New CSS Rule button.) The New CSS Rule dialog box opens. You'll create a level-one heading style.
Under Selector Type, select **Tag**	You'll define an element style, meaning that it will apply to all instances of a specific HTML tag.
In the Tag list, select **h1**	To apply this rule to the `<h1>` element.

4 In the Define in list, verify that globalstyles.css is selected	To define this style in the external style sheet, so that it will apply to all Web pages that are linked to that style sheet.
Click **OK**	The CSS Rule Definition dialog box appears.
5 Display the Size list	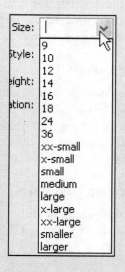
	To view a list of standard font sizes. You'll use a font size that doesn't appear in this list.
In the Size box, enter **22**	
	To enter the font size.
Click **OK**	The level-one heading in aboutus.html now appears in a 22-pixel font size.
6 Create a CSS rule	(Click the New CSS Rule button.) The New CSS Rule dialog box opens. You'll create a level-two heading style.
Create a rule for the **h2** element	Under Selector Type, click Tag. Then, in the Tag list, select h2.
Click **OK**	
7 In the Size list, select **18**	
Click **OK**	The level-two heading in aboutus.html now appears with an 18-pixel font size.
8 Activate globalstyles.css	Notice that the body rule now includes a font-size property, and that styles have been added for the h1 and h2 tags.
9 Save globalstyles.css	

Class styles

Explanation

You can create custom class styles, or classes, to accompany HTML element styles or to replace them. You can apply classes to any HTML element. For example, suppose that you want to apply a special format to one paragraph. If you changed the style definition for the <p> tag, the change would affect all paragraphs on pages with that style sheet attached. Instead, you can create a CSS class style with the desired format, and apply it to only the paragraph(s) where it's needed.

Class names

Class names must begin with a period (.). The period indicates that the style is a class style. Giving classes meaningful names will make maintenance easier, both for yourself and for others who might work on the site in the future. For example, a year from now, it will be easier to figure out where a class is used if it is named ".introNotes" instead of ".class2".

Creating class styles

As with element styles, you can place a class style in any of three locations: in a Web page, in an existing CSS style sheet, or in a new CSS style sheet.

To create a CSS class style:

1   Open one of the following:
    - A Web page (to create an internal class style that applies to only that page)
    - A style sheet, or a Web page that is linked to a style sheet (to create a class style in the external style sheet)
2   In the CSS Styles panel, click the New CSS Rule button.
3   In the New CSS Rule dialog box, under Selector type, select Class.
4   In the Name box, type a name that begins with a period (.).
5   Under Define in, do one of the following:
    - In the list, select a new or existing style sheet file.
    - Select This document only (to create the style in the active document).
6   Click OK.
7   In the CSS Rule Definition dialog box, define the attributes for the style.
8   Click OK.

Do it!

C-4: Creating class styles

Here's how	Here's why
1 Activate aboutus.html	You'll create a class style.
Create a CSS rule	(In the CSS Styles panel, click the New CSS Rule button.) The New CSS Rule dialog box opens.
Next to Selector Type, select **Class**	To begin creating a new class style.
In the Name box, enter **.leadPara**	To replace the default class name with a more meaningful and appropriate name. All class names begin with a period.
2 In the Define in list, verify that globalstyles.css is selected	To create this style in the external style sheet, so that the style will apply to all Web pages that are linked to the style sheet.
Click **OK**	
3 In the Size list, select **14**	To apply a font size of 14 pixels to the .leadPara class.
In the Weight list, select **bold**	To make text defined by the .leadPara class bold.
Click **OK**	
4 Create a class rule named **.copyright**	(Click the New CSS Rule button, type the name, and verify that Class is checked as the Selector Type. Then click OK.) You'll create a class to apply to the copyright text.
5 In the Size box, enter **11**	
From the Style list, select **italic**	
Click **OK**	Now that you've created the class style, you still need to apply it to specific elements on the page.
6 In the document window, scroll to the bottom of the page	
Click inside the copyright text	
7 In the Property inspector, in the Styles list, select **copyright**	To apply this class style to the text. The copyright statement changes to 11-pixel italic text.

8 Click [⊠ Split]	(The Show Code and Design Views button.) To display both Code view and Design view for the page.
Observe the code for the copyright text	`<div align="center" class="copyright">&copy; Outlar`
	The class style is applied using the `class` attribute.
Return to Design view	Click the Show Design view button.
9 In the CSS Styles panel, click [✎]	(The Edit Style button.) You'll edit the class style.
In the Category list, select **Background**	To specify background attributes for this rule.
10 Click the Background color box	A color palette appears, and the pointer changes to an eye dropper.
Select the green color **#99CC33**	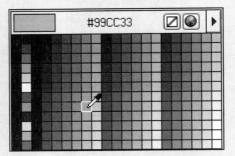
Click **OK**	The copyright text now has a green background that matches the navigation bar.
11 Click the copyright line	To select it.
In the Property inspector, click [CSS]	(The Open CSS Panel button.) To display the Current tab in the CSS Styles panel. If the CSS Panel group had been closed, clicking this button would open it.
12 In the CSS Styles panel, in the Summary for Selection list, point to **font-family**	A tooltip appears that describes this property of the copyright line.
	font-family Verdana, Geneva, . font-size 10px This property is set in rule "body" in file globalstyles.cs
Click **font-size**	You'll use the CSS Styles panel to edit globalstyles.css.

13 Under Properties for ".copyright", click **11 px**

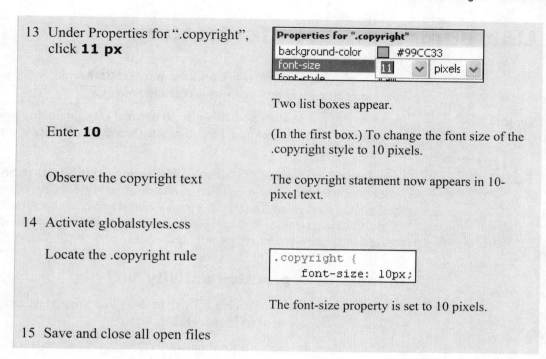

Two list boxes appear.

    Enter **10**

(In the first box.) To change the font size of the .copyright style to 10 pixels.

    Observe the copyright text

The copyright statement now appears in 10-pixel text.

14 Activate globalstyles.css

    Locate the .copyright rule

```
.copyright {
    font-size: 10px;
}
```

The font-size property is set to 10 pixels.

15 Save and close all open files

Unit summary: Text formatting

Topic A   In this topic, you changed **line breaks** to **paragraph breaks**. Then you learned how to insert **special characters** and **non-breaking spaces**.

Topic B   In this topic, you learned how to apply **structural tags**, including headings and paragraphs. Then, you learned how to create three kinds of **lists**: unordered lists, ordered lists, and nested lists.

Topic C   In this topic, you learned the basics of **Cascading Style Sheets (CSS)**. You learned about the differences between internal and external style sheets, basic CSS syntax, and the function of element styles, class styles, and ID styles. Then you learned how to create an external style sheet and link documents to it. Finally, you learned how to create and apply element styles and class styles.

Independent practice activity

In this activity, you will attach a CSS style sheet to a Web page, create and apply a class style, and create element styles for HTML tags.

1 Using the Files panel, open index.html from the outlanderspices.com folder in the Practice folder. (In the current unit folder.)

2 Attach globalstyles.css to index.html. (*Hint*: The external style sheet is in the styles folder.)

3 Apply the Heading 2 style to the text "In the News" and "Featured Product."

4 In globalstyles.css, create a class style named **.mission** that makes text bold, italic, and 14 pixels.

5 Apply the .mission style to the first paragraph in index.html.

6 Open recipes.html and attach globalstyles.css to it.

7 Define a new CSS style for the ul (unordered list) element.

8 Give the ul style a left margin of **25** pixels. Verify the changes in recipes.html. (*Hint*: In the CSS Rule Definition dialog box, select Box in the Category list. Below Margin, clear Same for all, and type 25 in the Left box.)

9 Define a new CSS style for the ol (ordered list) element with a left margin of 65 pixels. Verify the changes in recipes.html.

10 Save and close all open files.

Review questions

1 Structuring your documents in a meaningful, logical hierarchy of elements provides which benefits? (Choose all that apply.)

   A It helps to establish consistency throughout a page or a site.

   B It saves you time and effort when you later update a site.

   C It allows your pages to be indexed by search engines more efficiently.

   D It increases your site traffic.

   E It allows Dreamweaver to function optimally.

2 When you have a list of items that follow a particular sequence, you should format them in a(n):

A   Unordered list.

B   Ordered list.

C   Nested list.

D   Definition list.

3 If you want all the level-two headings on your site to have the same formatting, you should:

A   Create an internal element style for the `<h2>` tag.

B   Create an external element style for the `<h2>` tag.

C   Create an internal class style.

D   Create an external class style.

4 If you want to create a special type of paragraph with extra large text, and you think you'll need to use the style for multiple paragraphs on a page, it's best to:

A   Create an internal element style for the `<p>` tag.

B   Create an external element style for the `<p>` tag.

C   Create an external class style and give it a meaningful name.

D   Create an external ID style and give it a meaningful name.

5 If you want to define a unique section that holds the navigation bar, and you want this element to look the same on every page, it's best to:

A   Create an internal class style and give it a meaningful name, such as "navbar."

B   Create an external class style and give it a meaningful name, such as "navbar."

C   Create an internal ID style and give it a meaningful name, such as "navbar."

D   Create an external ID style and give it a meaningful name, such as "navbar."

Unit 4

Tables

Unit time: 60 minutes

Complete this unit, and you'll know how to:

A Insert an HTML table, and create a nested table.

B Format rows and cells, merge cells, and add rows and columns to a table.

C Set fixed and variable widths for tables and columns, and change cell borders and padding.

D Create a layout table to arrange page content.

Topic A: Creating tables

Explanation

A table is a grid structure of rows and columns that you can use to display tabular data, such as products and prices, or to arrange page elements. Tables can be nested inside other tables.

Table structure

HTML tables are considered structural elements and are generally meant for data that's best arranged in rows and columns, such as the information shown in Exhibit 4-1. You can use tables as layout tables—to arrange Web page components—but it's typically best to use CSS to achieve layout and style objectives.

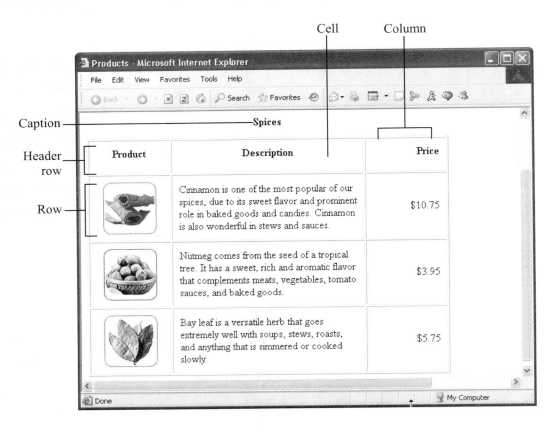

Exhibit 4-1: A simple table used to arrange content

HTML tables typically have *header rows* (rows with column headings) and can have captions. You can insert text and images in table cells (the intersections of columns and rows).

Inserting tables

To insert a table, drag the Table icon from the Common group on the Insert bar to the page. Then, define the basic table settings in the Table dialog box, as shown in Exhibit 4-2. You can then use the Property inspector to change table properties as necessary. After you have created a table, you can drag text and images to the cells as needed.

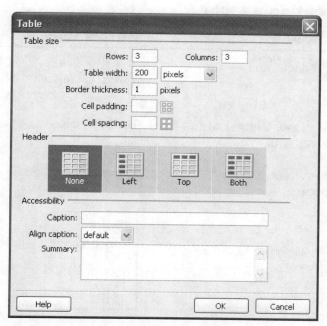

Exhibit 4-2: The Table dialog box

The following table describes the options available in the Table dialog box.

Option	Defines
Rows	The number of rows in the table.
Columns	The number of columns in the table.
Table width	The width of the table, either in pixels or as a percentage of the browser window or of a container, such as a layer or `<div>` tag.
Border thickness	The width of the cell borders.
Cell padding	The amount of space between a cell's contents and the cell's border.
Cell spacing	The amount of space between adjacent cells.
Header	The left column, the top row, or both, used as a heading.
Caption	A title that describes the table.
Align caption	The alignment of an optional table caption; you can align it to the top, bottom, left, or right of the table.
Summary	A description that can be read by screen readers for the visually impaired.

Do it!

A-1: Creating a table

Here's how	Here's why
1 Open products.html	(From the outlanderspices.com folder, in the current unit folder.) You'll create a table and add text and images to it.
2 Choose **View**, **Visual Aids**, **Table Widths**	To display table-width bars.
3 On the Insert bar, select **Common**	If necessary.
Drag [EE] to the document window, as shown	
	The Table dialog box appears.
In the Rows box, enter **4**	To set the number of table rows to four.
In the Columns box, enter **2**	To set the number of columns to two.
4 In the list next to the Table width box, verify that pixels is selected	To set the table width in pixels.
In the Table width box, enter **580**	To set the table width to 580 pixels.
Under Header, click **Top**	
	To make the top row of the table a header row.
5 In the Caption box, enter **Spices**	To create a table caption.
In the Align caption list, verify that default is selected	The default alignment for table caption is the top center.
6 In the Summary box, enter **Outlander spices and their descriptions**	To create a summary that describes this table for screen readers used by the visually impaired.
Click **OK**	

7 Double-click the caption text

In the Property inspector, click **B** — To make the caption text bold.

8 In the top row of the left column, type **Product** — To create a heading for this column. By default, the text in this row is bold and centered in each cell, because that's the default style of the `<th>` (table header) element, which defines each cell in this row. You can change these default styles with CSS, if necessary.

9 In the top row of the right column, type **Description** — To create a heading for the right column.

10 In the Files panel, navigate to the images folder — (In the outlanderspices.com folder, which is in the current unit folder.) You'll add images to the table.

Drag **cinnamon.jpg** to the cell under "Product" — The Image Tag Accessibility Attributes dialog box appears.

In the Alternate text box, enter **Cinnamon image** — To create alternate text for this image.

Click **OK** — To place the image and close the dialog box.

11 Insert **nutmeg.jpg** and **bayleaf.jpg** in the cells below cinnamon.jpg, as shown

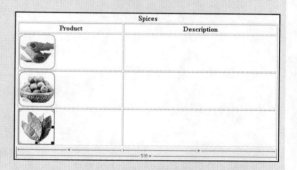

Drag the nutmeg image to its cell, specify appropriate alternate text, and click OK. Repeat for the bayleaf image.

12 Open descriptions.txt

You'll insert text from this file into the table.

Copy the descriptions of each spice into the corresponding cell in the Description column

Select each description, copy it, and paste it into the appropriate cell.

Close descriptions.txt

Delete any line breaks and spaces that appear at the end of each paragraph

Cinnamon is one of th
prominent role in bak
stews and sauces. [BR]

If necessary.

13 Save products.html

Preview the page in a browser

Close the browser

Nested tables

Explanation

A *nested table* is a table that's inserted in the cell of another table. Nested tables give you more flexibility in arranging content. For example, Exhibit 4-3 shows a nested table; the outer table contains all the content shown, and the nested table contains text in cells that will be used to create a navigation bar. The outer table consists of one column and two rows. The nested table is placed in the second row of the outer table and consists of one row and eight columns.

Exhibit 4-3: An example of a nested table used for layout purposes

A-2: Creating a nested table

Here's how	Here's why
1 Drag 🔲 to the top-left corner of the page, as shown	
	(From the Insert bar.) The Table dialog box appears. You'll create a nested table above the existing table.
2 Set the number of Rows to **2** and the number of Columns to **1**	In the Rows box, enter 2, and in the Columns box, enter 1.
Set the width to **780**	In the Table width box, enter 780.
Under Header, click **None**	You will not need a header row for this table.
3 In the Summary box, enter **Navigation bar**	To create a summary that describes this table. Table summaries provide a context for the table for users with alternative browsers like screen readers.
Click **OK**	
4 Insert **logo.jpg** in the top row	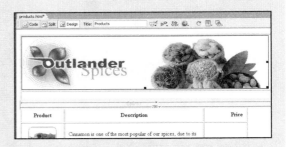
	In the Files panel, navigate to the images folder in the outlanderspices.com folder. Drag logo.jpg to the top row. Then, in the Image Tag Accessibility Attributes dialog box, enter alternate text and click OK.

5 Drag ⊞ to the bottom row of the table

To nest another table inside the existing table. The Table dialog box appears.

Set the number of Rows to **1** and the number of Columns to **8**

Set the Table width to **780**

Click **OK**

6 In the eight cells of the nested table, enter the following headings:
Home
About Us
Locations
Products
Recipes
Site Search
Order Online
Contact Us

As shown in Exhibit 4-3. These headings will eventually serve as navigation links.

7 Save products.html

Topic B: Changing table structure and formatting

Explanation

Now that you know how to create tables and add text and images to them, you'll want to know how to change the formatting and adjust a table's structure. To do that, you should be familiar with the various table-related tags and be able to select table components.

Selecting table components

In HTML, tables are defined by the `<table>` tag. Within that tag, each `<tr>` tag defines a row, and within a row, each `<td>` tag defines a cell. The number of cells in a row determines the number of columns in the table. For example, Exhibit 4-4 shows the code for a table consisting of two rows—notice the two sets of `<tr>` tags—and three columns. The resulting table is shown on the right.

```
<table>
    <tr>
        <td> </td>
        <td> </td>
        <td> </td>
    </tr>

    <tr>
        <td> </td>
        <td> </td>
        <td> </td>
    </tr>
</table>
```

Exhibit 4-4: A simple table

You can select all the cells in a column or row, or select individual cells. You need to select a row, column, or cell before you can set properties for it.

Selecting table cells

The easiest and fastest way to select an individual cell is to press Ctrl and click the cell. You can also click the cell and choose Edit, Select All, or you can click the cell and then click the rightmost `<td>` tag in the tag selector at the bottom of the window, as shown in Exhibit 4-5.

Exhibit 4-5: Click a cell's tag to select the cell

Selecting rows or columns

To select a row or column, do any of the following:

- Point to the left edge of the leftmost cell (for a row), or the top edge of the topmost cell (for a column.) When the pointer changes to a position arrow, click the edge of the cell.

- Click the left cell of a row and drag to the right, or click the top cell of a column and drag down.

- (Rows only) Click the cell, and then click the rightmost `<tr>` tag in the tag selector at the bottom of the window.

Formatting rows

After you select a row, you can expand the Property inspector to customize the row formatting, as shown in Exhibit 4-6.

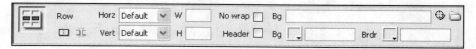

Exhibit 4-6: The Property inspector expands to display row formatting options

Using row formatting options, you can:

- Merge adjacent cells into a single continuous cell.
- Change the horizontal and vertical alignment of objects in the cells in the selected row.
- Change the width and height of the selected row.
- Allow the text in cells to wrap.
- Define the selected row as a table header row.
- Define a background image, background color, and border color.

Do it!

B-1:   Formatting rows

Here's how	Here's why
1 Point to the left edge of the top-left cell and click	![Product table with Cinnamon image] (Make sure the pointer changes to a right-pointing arrow before you click.) To select the row. You'll format this row.
2 In the lower-right corner of the Property inspector, click ▽	To expand the Property inspector.
In the H box, enter **30**	To set the row height to 30 pixels.
In the Vert list, select **Top**	To align the text to the top of the row.
3 Save products.html	

Modifying cells

Explanation

The Property inspector includes the same options for cells as it does for rows, with one exception. The cells in a row can be merged, but when a single cell is selected, you can also split it.

Cell width

When you change the width of a cell in a particular column, the entire column might be affected. Columns are sized according to their largest cell.

Background colors

You can specify a background color for rows, columns, and individual cells. To do so, select the row, column, or cell, and then click the Bg box in the Property inspector to open a color palette. Click a swatch to specify a color.

Inserting rows and columns

When a single cell is selected, you can add a row of cells above or below it, and you can add a column to the right or left of it.

To insert a row, do any of the following:

- Select a cell and choose Insert, Table Objects, Insert Row Above or Insert Row Below.
- Right-click a cell and choose Table, Insert Row. (The row will be inserted above the selected cell.)
- Right-click a cell and choose Table, Insert Rows or Columns. In the dialog box, apply the desired settings and click OK.

To insert a column, do any of the following:

- Select a cell and choose Insert, Table Objects, Insert Column to the Left or Insert Column to the Right.
- Right-click a cell and choose Table, Insert Column. (The column will be inserted to the left of the selected cell.)
- Right-click a cell and choose Table, Insert Rows or Columns. In the dialog box, apply the desired settings and click OK.

Do it!

B-2: Adding columns and rows and formatting cells

Here's how	Here's why
1 Click the cell containing "Description"	
2 Choose **Insert, Table Objects, Insert Column to The Right**	To add a column to the right of the selected cell.
3 Set the cell width to **100**	(In the W box in the Property inspector, enter 100.) To specify a width of 100 pixels. Changing the width of the cell affects the entire column. Column widths are set according to the largest cell in the column.

4 In the four new cells, enter **Price**, **$10.75**, **$3.95**, and **$5.75**

To create a column heading and enter the price data for the listed spices. Notice that the top cell in the new column is automatically formatted as a heading, like the other cells in this row.

5 Right-click any cell in the top row and choose **Table**, **Insert Row**

To insert a row at the top of the table.

Select the top row

Point to the left edge of the top-left cell in the Spices table until the pointer turns into an arrow, and then click.

Right-click the row and choose **Table**, **Merge Cells**

To merge the top row's cells into a single cell.

6 Click the merged cell

To place the insertion point in the cell.

Type **Featured Products**

7 In the Property inspector, click the Bg color box, as shown

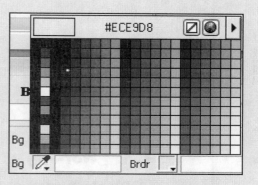

Select the dark green color **#006600**, as shown

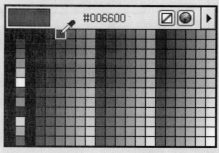

To give the cell a dark green background.

8 Select the text

Change the text to white

(In the Property inspector, click the Text Color box, and select white from the color picker.) To make the text more visible against the dark green background.

9 Save products.html

Topic C: Changing column width and cell properties

Explanation

You can further customize the appearance of tables by making column widths fixed or variable, along with specifying their sizes, and by hiding or modifying cell borders.

Fixed and variable widths for columns and tables

You can set a column's width to a fixed number of pixels or to a percentage of the table width. Similarly, you can set a table's width to either fixed or variable. A variable-width table is sized with a percentage value and is relative to the width of the browser window. You can also combine fixed- and variable-width settings, as described in the following table.

Column width	Table width	Resulting column width
100 pixels	500 pixels	100 pixels
100 pixels	85% of browser	100 pixels
10% (of table)	500 pixels	50 pixels (10% of 500 pixels)
10% (of table)	85% (of browser)	8.5% of browser (10% of 85%)

Do it!

C-1: Working with fixed and variable widths

Here's how	Here's why
1 Preview products.html in your browser	You'll change some of the columns from fixed widths to variable widths.
Point to the right edge of the browser window, as shown	
	The pointer changes to a double-sided arrow to enable resizing.
Drag the right edge of the window back and forth	To resize the window. Notice that the Products table remains the same size because it has a fixed width, so its size is not calculated relative to the size of the browser window.
Close the browser	

2 Select the cell containing
   "Product"

   In the W box, enter **100**   (In the Property inspector.) To set the width of
                                                the first column to 100 pixels.

3 Right-click the Products table and   (To select the entire table.) You'll change the
   choose **Table**, **Select Table**   width of the table from a fixed width to a
                                                percentage of the browser window. The options
                                                in the Property inspector change with the
                                                selection.

   In the W box, enter **85**

   In the list next to the W box,
   select **%**

                                                To make the table width 85% of the width of the
                                                browser window.

4 Click the cell containing "Home"   (In the nested table containing the navigation bar
                                                at the top of the page.) You'll apply a variable
                                                width to cells (columns) in this row.

   Select the row   Drag to the far-right cell in the row.

   In the W box, enter **12%**   (In the Property inspector.) To give the cells in
                                                this row a width of 12% of the table's width.

5 Select the Price column   (In the Spices table.) You'll align the price data
                                                in this column.

   In the Property inspector,   (The Align Right button.) To align the data in
   click ▤   these cells to the right.

6 Center the spice images in their   Select the column and click Align Center in the
   cells   Property inspector.

7 Save products.html

   Preview the results in your
   browser

   Resize the window   Drag the edge of the window back and forth.
                                                The Spices table expands and contracts as the
                                                window changes size. However, the right
                                                column of the Products table remains the same
                                                size because it still has a fixed width.

   Close the browser window

Borders and cell padding

Explanation
When you create a table, table borders are displayed by default. This makes it easier for you to see the columns and rows while you're building the table and working with the table content.

Default settings also apply to the spacing inside cells, to horizontal and vertical alignment, and to other formatting options. Depending on the purpose of your table, you might not want to display the table borders, or you might want to change the spacing between cells or change the spacing between cell content and cell borders. If you create a table for layout purposes, to arrange elements on a page, you'll probably want to disable the table borders, so that the layout framework is not visible.

Exhibit 4-7 shows two versions of the same table. The first uses the default settings for cell borders and cell spacing. In the second table, the borders are disabled, and the spacing inside the cells is increased. This spacing, between a cell's borders and its content, is called *cell padding*. You can change the amount of cell padding in the Cell Pad box in the Property inspector.

Featured Products		
Product	Description	Price
	Cinnamon is one of the most popular of our spices, due to its sweet flavor and prominent role in baked goods and candies. Cinnamon is also wonderful in stews and sauces.	$10.75
	Nutmeg comes from the seed of a tropical tree. It has a sweet, rich and aromatic flavor that complements meats, vegetables, tomato sauces, and baked goods.	$3.95
	Bay leaf is a versatile herb that goes extremely well with soups, stews, roasts, and anything that is simmered or cooked slowly.	$5.75

Featured Products		
Product	Description	Price
	Cinnamon is one of the most popular of our spices, due to its sweet flavor and prominent role in baked goods and candies. Cinnamon is also wonderful in stews and sauces.	$10.75
	Nutmeg comes from the seed of a tropical tree. It has a sweet, rich and aromatic flavor that complements meats, vegetables, tomato sauces, and baked goods.	$3.95
	Bay leaf is a versatile herb that goes extremely well with soups, stews, roasts, and anything that is simmered or cooked slowly.	$5.75

Exhibit 4-7: Two tables with different settings for borders and cell padding

Do it!   **C-2:   Customizing cell properties**

Here's how	Here's why
1 Select the Products table	You'll adjust the cell padding and borders.
2 Set the CellPad value to **10**	(In the Property inspector.) To increase the cell padding—the space between each cell's border and contents—to 10 pixels.
3 Set the Border value to **0**	To disable the table borders.
4 At the top of the page, select the outer table and disable its borders	
5 Save products.html	
View the results in a browser	The table borders no longer appear.
Close the browser window	
Close products.html	

Topic D: Working with layout tables

Explanation

In Dreamweaver's Layout mode, you can use tables to create page layouts. You can also place multiple layout tables on a page. By doing this, you can customize the table grid and properties of one layout section without affecting other sections.

Creating layout tables

To create a layout table:

1 On the Insert bar, select the Layout menu.
2 Select Layout mode.
3 On the Insert bar, click the Layout Table button.
4 Point to an empty area of the document. When the pointer changes to a crosshair, click the page.
5 Using the Property inspector, resize and format the layout table as needed.

Do it!   ### D-1:   Creating a layout table

Here's how	Here's why
1 Open aboutus.html	You'll create a layout for this page by using layout tables.
2 Click the Insert bar and select the **Layout** menu, as shown	
	To display the Layout items.
On the Insert bar, click **Layout**	
	To switch to Layout mode. The Getting Started in Layout Mode dialog box appears.
Click **OK**	
Choose **View**, **Visual Aids**, **Hide All**	To hide the visual aids for the layout tables.
3 Click	(The Layout Table button is on the Insert bar.) To start a layout table.
Point to the blank area below the Home button, as shown	
	The pointer changes to a crosshair.
Click the page	To place a blank layout table at this position.
4 In the Property inspector, in the Width box, enter **780**	To apply a fixed width of 780 pixels.
In the Height box, enter **1638**	
	To apply a height of 1638 pixels.
5 Save aboutus.html	

Using layout cells

Explanation
You can resize layout cells and drag them to specific positions within a table. This allows text, images, and other objects inserted in those cells to be positioned precisely where you need them on a Web page. This is typically easier than creating a complicated series of nested tables. Exhibit 4-8 shows an example of a layout table and individual layout cells.

To insert a layout cell:

1 On the Insert bar, select the Layout menu.
2 Select Layout mode (if necessary.)
3 On the Insert bar, click the Draw Layout Cell button.
4 Drag on the page to create a layout cell.
5 Drag the cell to position it exactly where you need it.
6 Resize and format the cell as needed by using the Property inspector.

If you drag within a layout table, Dreamweaver inserts the cell in that table. If you drag on a blank area of the page, Dreamweaver automatically creates a new layout table to hold the cell.

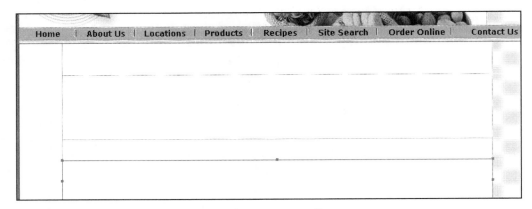

Exhibit 4-8: A layout table and individual layout cells

Do it!

D-2: Working with layout cells

Here's how	Here's why
1 Click	(The Draw Layout Cell button is on the Insert bar.) You'll add layout cells to the layout table to act as containers and to provide spacing.
Drag inside the layout table, as shown	
	To create a layout cell within the existing layout table.
Click an edge of the layout cell	To select it.
2 Drag the layout cell past the border of the layout table	
	The pointer changes to indicate that you cannot drag to this location.
Release the mouse	The layout cell snaps back to its original position. You can't move the layout cell to a position where it overlaps or collides with another table object.
3 Drag the layout cell to the top-left corner of the layout table	
Click the border of the layout cell	(If necessary.) To select it.

4 Set the Width to **65** and the Height to **1638**

In the Property inspector.

5 Draw another layout cell and position it next to the first, as shown

Click the Draw Layout Cell button on the Insert bar. Then drag in the layout table and drag the new layout cell to the corner.

Set the Width to **648** and the Height to **50**

6 Insert a new layout cell at the corner where the first two layout cells meet, as shown

Set the Width to **648** and the Height to **100**

7 Add another layout cell with a Width of **648** and a Height of **33**

8 Add another layout cell with a Width of **648** and a Height of **840**

The table should look like the one shown in Exhibit 4-8.

9 Save aboutus.html

Adding content to layout cells

Explanation

You can add text, images, and other page elements to a layout cell. To add text, an image, or another asset from a file to a cell:

1   Drag the file from the Files panel to the layout cell.
2   Resize and reposition the layout cell as needed.

Do it!

D-3:   Adding content to a layout table

Here's how	Here's why
1 In the Files pane, navigate to the images folder	(In the current unit folder.) You'll add text and images to the layout table you created.
2 Drag **aboutus.jpg** to the second layout cell from the top In the Alternate Text box, type **About us** Click **OK**	The Image Tag Accessibility Attributes dialog box appears.
	The image is displayed, as shown here.
3 Drag **heading-allspicedup.gif** to the next layout cell In the Alternate Text box, type **All Spiced Up** Click **OK**	The Image Tag Accessibility Attributes dialog box appears.
Click the border of the layout cell	To select it.
In the Property inspector, in the Vert list, select **Bottom**	
	To align the image with the bottom of the layout cell.

4 Drag **aboutus.txt** to the next layout cell	To insert text in the page. The Insert Document dialog box opens.
Click **Insert the Contents**	If necessary.
Click **Text only** and click **OK**	To insert the text from the file and close the dialog box.
On the Insert bar, click **Standard**	Standard │ Expanded │ Layout
	To switch to Standard mode.
5 Save aboutus.html	
Preview the page in your browser	
Close the browser	
6 Close all open files	

Unit summary: Tables

Topic A   In this topic, you learned about **tables**. You learned how to insert a table, create a header row, insert text and images, and create **nested tables**.

Topic B   In this topic, you learned how to **select and format** cells, rows, and columns. You also learned how to merge cells and insert rows and columns.

Topic C   In this topic, you learned how to fine-tune **table properties**, including column and table widths, cell borders, and cell padding.

Topic D   In this topic, you learned how to create a **layout table** and add layout cells. You learned how to arrange cells, change their dimensions, and insert content.

Independent practice activity

In this activity, you'll create a nested table and add images and text to it, add rows to an existing table, and place a layout table and layout cells on a page.

1 From the outlanderspices.com folder in the Practice folder (in the current unit folder), open locations.html.

2 Below the navigation bar, create a table with three rows, one column, and a width of 580 pixels.

3 Make sure the table border is disabled.

4 In the top row, insert the image usa-map.gif and center it. (*Hint*: The file is located in the images folder. Resize the image if desired.)

5 In the bottom row, insert a nested table with four rows and two columns, and center it.

6 Make the nested table 475 pixels wide, with a left column that's 175 pixels wide, and a right column that's 300 pixels wide.

7 Give the nested table a cell padding of **10**.

8 Add the text shown in Exhibit 4-9. (*Hint*: Use the Property inspector to format the text and the cells.)

9 Above Nevada, add a row for Oregon with the following locations:
   • Shopper's Paradise, Portland
   • Port Plaza, Santa Barbara

10 Open sitemap.html. As shown in Exhibit 4-10, create a layout table with layout cells, and insert search.jpg.

11 Save and close all open files.

STATE	STORES AND LOCATIONS
Washington	• Seattle Blue Heaven • Sierra Foods, Medford
Nevada	• All U Need, Reno • Plaza Givo, Las Vegas
California	• Shopper's Paradise, Los Angeles • Shopping Plaza, San Diego

Exhibit 4-9: The locations.html Web page as it appears after Step 8

Exhibit 4-10: The sitemap.html Web page as it appears after Step 10

Review questions

1 A nested table is:

   A A table that's inserted into a row of another table

   B A table that's inserted into a cell of another table

   C A table with fixed dimensions

   D A table with flexible dimensions

2 The number of columns in a table is determined by:

   A The number of rows

   B The number of column tags

   C The number of cells in each row

   D The value of the column attribute

3 The width of a column is determined by:

   A The width you set for the first cell in the column

   B The width you set for the table

   C The width you set for an intersecting row

   D The width of the largest cell in that column

4 A table has a fixed width of 600 pixels. A cell inside this table has a width of 20%, and no other width is specified for another cell in its column. How many pixels wide is this column?

   A 80 pixels

   B 60 pixels

   C 160 pixels

   D 180 pixels

   E 120 pixels

5 Cell padding is:

   A The space between a cell's borders and content

   B The space between cells

   C The space between rows and columns

   D The space between a table and the bottom of the page

Unit 5

Images

Unit time: 30 minutes

Complete this unit, and you'll know how to:

A Choose appropriate image formats, create text images, and modify image properties.

B Insert background images and resize images.

Topic A: Image formats and tags

Explanation

Images are an integral part of Web design. They catch the user's eye, they can introduce a unique artistic aspect to site designs, and they can often deliver information in a way that text cannot. For example, images of products give potential buyers visual information that can't be matched by a text description.

Images on the Web

File size is a vital consideration when using images on Web pages. Large image files can take a long time to load in a user's browser. Try to keep your image file sizes as small as possible without sacrificing quality.

You can find images for your Web site from a variety of sources, including the following:

- Some Web sites offer free images for downloading. Make sure that you read the site's downloading policy before you use any free images. Unauthorized use of images usually qualifies as copyright infringement.
- You can purchase image collections on CD-ROM or directly from Web sites.
- You can create your own images. For example, you can take digital photos and then use a program such as Adobe Photoshop to modify and optimize your images for the Web. You can also create images that are not based on a photograph. Adobe Photoshop and Illustrator are two popular programs that enable you to create your own Web graphics.

File formats

The three main image formats currently supported by browsers are GIF, JPEG, and PNG. GIF images, which can contain a maximum of 256 colors, are best used for images with relatively few colors and with areas of flat color, such as line drawings, logos, and illustrations. GIFs also support animation and transparency. The GIF format is not recommended for photographs or illustrations with complex color gradations. When you save simple images of fewer than 256 colors, GIF uses a *lossless* compression algorithm, which means that no image data is discarded to compress the image.

The JPEG format supports more than 16 million colors, so it's best for photographs and images that have many subtle color shadings. JPEG uses *lossy* compression, which means that some image data is discarded when the file is saved. You can select the degree of compression applied when saving the file, with the following tradeoff: the smaller the file, the lower the image quality.

The PNG format combines some of the best features of JPEG and GIF. It supports more than 16 million colors, so it's ideal for photos and complex drawings. It can use a variety of lossless compression algorithms, and it supports many levels of transparency, allowing areas of an image to appear transparent or semi-transparent. The downside of PNG is that some browsers do not support it. The following table summarizes these three image file formats.

	GIF	JPEG	PNG
Best used for:	Simple images with few colors	Photographs	Photographs or simple images
Maximum colors	256	More than 16 million	More than 16 million
Compression	Lossless	Lossy	Lossless
Transparency	One level (complete transparency)	Not supported	Multiple levels
Browser support	All	All	Netscape 6 and later, Internet Explorer 7 and later, Firefox, Safari

Do it!

A-1:   Discussing image formats

Questions	Answers
1 Which image formats are best for photographs?	
2 Which image formats support transparency?	
3 Why should you be careful when using the PNG format?	
4 True or false: The GIF format and JPEG format support the same number of colors	
5 A corporate logo that contains text and six colors is probably best saved in what image format?	

Image-based text

Explanation

You can add text to a page in the form of an image. If you have a graphics application such as Adobe Photoshop, Adobe Illustrator, or Macromedia Fireworks, you can type text into a graphic and save it with the appropriate file extension. Image-based text is often used for logos or for headings that require special styling that can't be provided by HTML or CSS.

By using image-based text, you can also use exotic fonts that your users are not likely to have on their machines and would therefore be unable to display otherwise. You might also want to apply special effects such as drop shadows or embossing, which you can't create by using actual text.

Image-based text also has its disadvantages. Images increase a page's overall size and download time. Using too many of these images can make a page exceedingly slow for some users. Also, because the images are not text, the content is not searchable by search engines, like Google, or by the browser's Find function. You can minimize this limitation by always specifying alternate text for your images.

Do it!

A-2:   Inserting images

Here's how	Here's why
1 Open recipes.html	From the outlanderspices.com folder, in the current unit folder. You'll replace the title of each recipe with a graphic that has a drop-shadow effect.
2 Delete **Princely Potatoes**	Select the text and press Delete.
Expand the Files panel	(If necessary.) To display the files and folders.
Navigate to the images folder	In the outlanderspices.com folder, in the current unit folder.
3 Drag **heading-potatoes.gif** to the recipes.html window	(From the images folder.) The Image Tag Accessibility Attributes dialog box appears.
In the Alternate text box, type **Princely Potatoes**	To give this image alternate text that matches the image's content, so that search engines can index the text.
Click **OK**	To close the dialog box and insert the image.
4 Place the graphic as shown	

This image will serve as the new heading for the Princely Potatoes recipe.

5 Delete **Chicken Stuffed with Spices**	
Make **heading-chicken.gif** the new heading	Drag the image above the recipe, on the same line as the Princely Potatoes heading. In the Image Tag Accessibility Attributes dialog box, enter appropriate alternate text and click OK.
6 Save recipes.html	

Image attributes

Explanation

When you drag an image onto a page, Dreamweaver writes the HTML code required to embed the image. This code consists of the `<img>` (image) tag and several *attributes*, which are properties for the element. The location of the `<img>` tag tells the browser where to embed the file, and the `src` attribute tells the browser where to locate the image file. The attributes of the `<img>` tag are described in the following table.

Attribute	Use is...	Description
src	Required	Specifies the URL or path to the image file.
alt	Recommended	Specifies alternate text. If the browser can't display the image, alternate text allows access to the text in the image, or a description of the image, whichever is most appropriate.
height	Recommended	Specifies the height of the image.
width	Recommended	Specifies the width of the image.
align	Optional	Aligns an image with text on the same line.
border	Optional	Specifies the pixel width of the border around an image that acts as a link.
hspace	Optional	Specifies the space, in pixels, to the left and right of the image.
vspace	Optional	Specifies the space, in pixels, above and below the image.

Image properties

The `<img>` tag's attributes and other image properties are defined with the Property inspector. The options shown in Exhibit 5-1 appear in the Property inspector when you select an image.

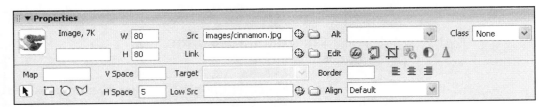

Exhibit 5-1: The Property inspector when an image is selected

Alternate text

You should always create alternate text for your images so that users with alternative devices such as screen readers or Braille devices can access the text content of an image or its description or context in the page. You've already entered alternate text when embedding an image for the first time. If you're dealing with an image that has already been added to a page, you can select the image and then enter alternate text in the Alt box in the Property inspector.

In some browsers, including Internet Explorer, alternate text appears as a ScreenTip when you point to the image, as shown in Exhibit 5-2.

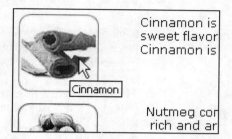

Exhibit 5-2: Alternate text is displayed as a ScreenTip in some browsers

A-3:   Modifying image properties

Here's how	Here's why
1 Select the image shown	
	You'll specify alternate text for this image.
In the Property inspector, click ▽	(If necessary. The expander button is in the lower-right corner.) To expand the Property inspector.
In the Alt box, enter **Princely Potatoes photo**	There is no text in this image, so it's best to provide a brief description of its contents.
2 Apply alternate text to the other recipe image	Select the image, and then enter an appropriate description in the Alt box in the Property inspector.
3 Select the Princely Potatoes heading	
	You'll increase the space between the recipe pictures and their headings.
In the V Space box, enter **15**	(In the Property inspector.) To add 15 pixels of space above and below the heading image.
4 Add 15 pixels of vertical space to the other heading image	Select the image, and enter 15 in the V Space box in the Property inspector.
5 Save recipes.html	
6 Preview the page in your browser	
Point to any image	A ScreenTip displays the alternate text you specified.
Close the browser	

Topic B: Backgrounds and image size

Explanation

You can use images as background illustrations for an element, such as a table, or for an entire Web page.

Background images

Background images repeat across and downward to occupy the element's entire dimensions. This repetition is called *tiling*. If you're working with a background image for an entire page, the image may tile several times to occupy the space—depending on the size of the image relative to the size of the browser window.

For example, if the image of peppers shown in Exhibit 5-3 is inserted as a background for a table, the image will tile to fill the width and height of the table, as shown in Exhibit 5-4. When selecting a background image, choose one that will not detract from the foreground of the page or make the text difficult to read. For example, the descriptions and prices in Exhibit 5-4 are difficult to read against the underlying peppers.

You can prevent an image from tiling so that it appears only once on the page, table, or other page element. You can also specify that the image tile only horizontally or only vertically.

Exhibit 5-3: An example of a background image

Product	Description	Price
	Cinnamon is one of the most popular of our spices, due to its sweet flavor and prominent role in baked goods and candies. Cinnamon is also wonderful in stews and sauces.	$10.75
	Nutmeg comes from the seed of a tropical tree. It has a sweet, rich and aromatic flavor that complements meats, vegetables, tomato sauces, and baked goods .	$3.95
	Bay leaf is a versatile herb goes extremely well with soups, stews, roasts, and anything that is simmered or cooked slowly.	$5.75

Exhibit 5-4: A small image used as a table background, tiling in both directions

To apply a background image to a page:

1 Click anywhere on the page.

2 In the Property inspector, click Page Properties to open the Page Properties dialog box.

3 In the Category list, select Appearance.

4 Click Browse to open the Select Image Source dialog box.

5 Navigate to the desired image file and click OK.

6 Click OK to close the Page Properties dialog box and apply the background image.

To apply a background image to a layout table:

1 Select the layout table.

2 In the Tag Inspector panel group, in the Attributes panel, expand the Browser specific attribute group.

3 Click the value for background.

4 Drag the Point-to-File icon to an image file in the Files panel, or click the Browse button and navigate to an image file.

To apply a background image to an ordinary HTML table:

1 Click in the table.

2 Expand the Property inspector (if necessary).

3 Drag the Point-to-File icon next to the BG Image box to an image file in the Files panel, or click the Browse button and navigate to an image file.

Do it!   **B-1:   Applying a background image**

Here's how	Here's why
1 In the Files panel, expand the images folder	You'll apply a background image to a table.
2 In recipes.html, click anywhere in the cell that contains "Home"	
Click the leftmost **\<table>** tag	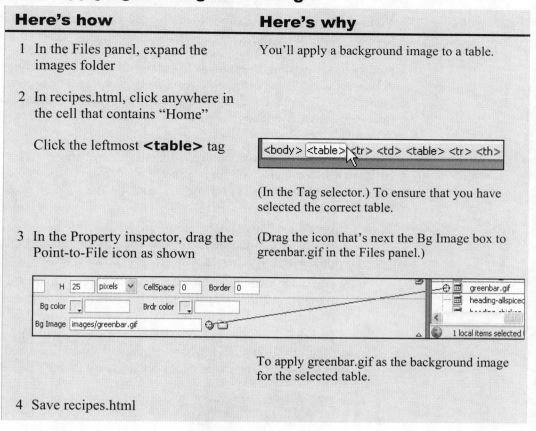
	(In the Tag selector.) To ensure that you have selected the correct table.
3 In the Property inspector, drag the Point-to-File icon as shown	(Drag the icon that's next the Bg Image box to greenbar.gif in the Files panel.)
	To apply greenbar.gif as the background image for the selected table.
4 Save recipes.html	

Image size

Explanation
You can change the dimensions of an image by specifying values in the W and H boxes in the Property inspector. ("W" is short for width, and "H" is short for height.) Most often, you'll want to simply specify the *actual* dimensions of an image, rather than modify its dimensions. Text loads faster than images, so specifying an image's actual dimensions allows the browser to load the page faster. The browser creates a "placeholder" that matches the image's size and loads other page content while the image downloads. When you embed an image, its actual height and width appear in the W and H boxes automatically.

Although you *can* adjust an image's dimensions by using the W and H boxes, it's much better to do your image editing in a program such as Adobe Photoshop, Adobe Illustrator, or Macromedia Fireworks. Using the W and H boxes to resize an image has the following drawbacks:

- Unless you change both settings proportionally, the image will get distorted. For example, if an image is 275 pixels wide by 344 pixels high, and you change the width to 290, you must set the height to 362 to retain the proportions.
- If you enlarge the image too much, it will appear pixilated. The square pixels that make up an image become large enough to be seen individually, as demonstrated in Exhibit 5-5.
- If you shrink the image too much, image quality will suffer, and it might be difficult for users to tell what the image is. In addition, reducing the image's dimensions in this manner does not decrease its file size.

Exhibit 5-5: Enlarged, original, and reduced versions of an image

Do it!
B-2: Resizing images

Here's how	Here's why
1 Select the indicated image	
2 In the H box, enter **50**	(In the Property inspector.) To decrease the height of the image to 50 pixels.
3 Observe the image	
	The image appears distorted, which is usually not the desired effect.

4 Click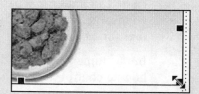

(The Reset size button is in the Property inspector. This button appears only if you change the width or height.) The image returns to its original size. You'll resize the image proportionally.

5 Point to the handle in the lower-right corner of the image, as shown

The pointer changes to a double-sided diagonal arrow.

Press and hold (SHIFT)

To force the image to resize proportionally as you drag.

Drag up until the H box in the Property inspector reads **50**

Release (SHIFT)

The image is resized proportionally.

6 Click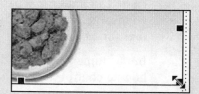

To return the image to its original size.

7 If you want to decrease the size of an image, should you use the W and H boxes?

8 Save and close recipes.html

Unit summary: Images

Topic A   In this topic, you learned about the **GIF**, **JPEG**, and **PNG** image formats. You learned the advantages and disadvantages of using image-based text, and you learned how to embed an image in a page. Then you learned about the **attributes** of the image tag, and you learned how to modify image properties. You also learned how to specify **alternate text** for an image.

Topic B   In this topic, you learned how to apply an image as a **background**. You also learned how to control the **height** and **width** of an image, and you learned about the drawbacks of resizing an image outside of an image-editing application.

Independent practice activity

In this activity, you will replace text with text images and add backgrounds to tables.

1   In the outlanderspices.com folder in the Practice folder (in the current unit folder), open aboutus.html.

2   Replace the text "All Spiced Up" with heading-allspicedup.gif. Enter appropriate alternate text for the image, and set the vertical space to 15. Check your results against Exhibit 5-6.

3   Replace the text "Expansion project" with heading-expansion.gif. Create appropriate alternate text, and set the vertical space to 15.

4   Apply greenbar.gif as the background for the second row in the top table, as shown in Exhibit 5-7.

5   Save and close aboutus.html.

Exhibit 5-6: The "All Spiced Up" heading after Step 2

Exhibit 5-7: The topbar.gif background after Step 4

Review questions

1 Which of the following are advantages of using image-based text? (Choose all that apply.)

   A Image-based text allows you to use exotic fonts and text effects.

   B Image-based text loads faster than normal text.

   C Image-based text can be more eye-catching than normal text.

   D Image-based text is easier to read than normal text.

2 If you want to increase the space around an image, you can:

   A Enter a numeric value in the V Space and H Space boxes.

   B Increase the height and width of the image.

   C Insert non-breaking spaces around the image.

   D Place the image in a table.

3 Alternate text for image-based text should:

   A Describe the content of the image.

   B Duplicate the text that appears in the image.

   C Be omitted.

   D Provide more information about the text.

4 Alternate text for a photograph should:

   A Describe the content of the image.

   B Duplicate any text that appears in the image.

   C Be omitted.

   D Merely indicate that it's a photographic image.

5 When you insert a background image, by default the image:

   A Tiles horizontally.

   B Tiles vertically.

   C Tiles horizontally and vertically.

   D Tiles diagonally.

Unit 6

Links

Unit time: 45 minutes

Complete this unit, and you'll know how to:

A Create links to other pages and resources, create named anchors and link to them, and create e-mail links.

B Create an image map.

C Apply CSS styles to link states.

Topic A: Creating links

Explanation

Links provide the functionality that makes the Web the interconnected world that it is. Links enable users to navigate to other pages in a site, to external pages and resources, and to specific sections of a page.

Link destinations and types

When a user clicks a link, the browser navigates to the destination specified in the link. You can set a link to open in the current browser window or a new browser window. These destination types are called link *targets*.

- A *Self* target opens the link destination in the current window.
- A *Blank* target opens the link destination in a new window.

Link types

There are three basic link types:

- *Local* links navigate to other pages and resources in a Web site.
- *External* links navigate to pages and resources outside a Web site.
- *Named-anchor* links navigate to specific sections of a Web page. Named-anchor links are also called *bookmark links* or *intra-document links*.

Local links

Local links are links to pages and resources within a Web site, so specifying the path is relatively simple. If the destination file resides in the same directory as the page that contains the link, you can simply type the file name in the Link box in the Property inspector. If the link destination resides in a different folder, you need to specify the folder, followed by the file name.

To create a local link:

1 Select the text or image that you want to serve as the link.
2 In the Property inspector, do one of the following:
   - Next to the Link box, drag the Point-to-File icon to the destination file in the Files panel.
   - Click the Browse button and navigate to the destination file.

Do it!   **A-1:   Creating a link to a page in your site**

Here's how	Here's why
1 Open aboutus.html	From the outlanderspices.com folder in the current unit folder.
2 Select **Home**	(In the navigation bar at the top of the page.) You'll create a link that navigates to the Home page.
3 In the Property inspector, click the folder icon as shown	
	(The Browse for File icon is to the right of the Link box.) To specify the path of the link target. The Select File dialog box appears.
4 Select **index.html**	(From the outlanderspices.com folder in the current unit folder.) To specify the link target.
Click **OK**	The word "Home" is now a link. By default, a link appears as blue, underlined text to distinguish it from normal text.
5 Save aboutus.html	
6 Preview the page in your browser	To see the link in action.
Click **Home**	The browser navigates to index.html.
Close the browser	

Named anchors

Explanation

Named anchors can mark any HTML element on a Web page as a target, so that any link navigates directly to that position on the page. This is useful for long pages, as an alternative to scrolling. You can also link to a named anchor on another page in your site.

To create a named anchor:

1 Choose View, Visual Aids, Invisible Elements (if necessary) so that named-anchor tags will appear in the document window.
2 Place the insertion point at the target location.
3 On the Insert bar, select Common and then click the Named Anchor button. The Named Anchor dialog box appears.
4 In the Anchor Name box, type a name for the anchor.
5 Click OK.

To link to a named anchor, select the text or image that will serve as the link. Then, in the Property inspector, do one of the following:

- In the Link box, type # (the number sign), followed immediately by the name of the anchor: #*anchorName*.
- Drag the Point-to-File icon beside the Link box to the named anchor.

Do it!

A-2: Creating and linking to a named anchor

Here's how	Here's why
1 Choose **View**, **Visual Aids**, **Invisible Elements**	(If necessary.) To display invisible elements, including symbols for named anchors. You'll insert a named anchor and create a link to it.
Place the insertion point at the top of the page	Click the blank line below the navigation bar.
On the Insert bar, select **Common**	(If necessary.) To display the common insert items.
2 Click [icon]	(The Named Anchor button.) The Named Anchor dialog box appears.
In the Anchor Name box, enter **top**	
Click **OK**	The anchor symbol appears.
3 Click the blank line above the copyright statement	(At the bottom of the page.) To place the insertion point at this location.
Type **Go to Top**	
4 Select **Go to Top**	You'll make this text a link to the *top* anchor.
In the Property inspector, in the Link box, type **#top**	
5 Save aboutus.html	
6 Preview the page in your browser	To see the link in action.
Scroll to the bottom of the page and click **Go to Top**	The browser navigates to the named anchor at the top of the page.
Close the browser	
Close aboutus.html	
7 How might you use named anchors in your own Web site?	

External links

Explanation

External links navigate to a page or resource on another Web site. You can also create a link that launches the user's default e-mail program, begins an outgoing message, and inserts the e-mail address of your choice in the To field.

To create an external link:

1   Select the text or image that you want to serve as the link.
2   In the Property inspector, in the Link box, type the complete URL to the destination page or resource.

To create an e-mail link:

1   Select the text or image that you want to serve as the link.
2   In the Property inspector, in the Link box, type **mailto:** followed by the e-mail address to which you want the message to be sent.

If no e-mail application is configured on the user's computer when an e-mail link is clicked, a dialog box appears, prompting the user to configure an e-mail application.

Do it!

A-3:   Creating external links and e-mail links

Here's how	Here's why
1 Open index.html	(In the outlanderspices.com folder, in the current unit folder.) You'll create an external link and an e-mail link.
2 Select the ISO 9000 award image	You'll make this image an external link.
3 In the Link box, type **http://www.iso.org**	In the Property inspector.
Press (↵ ENTER)	The image is now a link to the specified URL.
4 Select **Contact Us**	(In the page's navigation bar.) You'll make this text an e-mail link.
In the Link box, type **mailto:info@outlanderspices.com**	
Press (↵ ENTER)	When the user clicks the link, his or her default e-mail program will open, with this address used for the outgoing message.
5 Save index.html	
6 Preview the page in your browser	
7 Click **Contact Us**	An e-mail message with the specified address opens in the default e-mail application. (If no e-mail application is configured on the computer, you are prompted to configure an e-mail application.)
Close the e-mail message	If applicable.
Click the ISO 9000 award image	To view the ISO Web site.
Close the browser	
8 Close index.html	

Topic B: Creating image maps

Explanation

An *image map* is an image that contains multiple links. Different areas within the image, called *hotspots*, are linked to various targets.

Hotspots

A hotspot in an image map can be any size and can be any of several shapes: oval, circle, rectangle, square, or irregularly shaped polygon.

To create an image map:

1 Select the image in the document window.

2 Expand the Property inspector (if necessary).

3 In the Map Name box, enter a unique name for the image map.

4 Click the Rectangular Hotspot Tool, the Oval Hotspot Tool, or the Polygon Hotspot Tool.

5 Drag to draw the outline, or, if you're using the Polygon tool, click the corners of the shape to begin the outline.

6 Use the Point-to-File icon or the Browse button next to the Link box to link to a local link, a named anchor, or an external link.

Do it!

B-1: Creating an image map

Here's how	Here's why
1 Open locations.html	
Click the image of the U.S.	To select it.
In the Property inspector, click ▽	(If necessary.) To expand the Property inspector.
2 Click ▱	The Rectangular Hotspot Tool is in the Property inspector.
3 Point to **OR**, as shown	
	(The pointer changes to a crosshair.) You'll insert a hotspot here so that when a user clicks Oregon, the browser will jump to the specified destination.
Drag over and down to draw a rectangle, as shown	
	This will define the clickable region for this link.
4 Observe the Link box	(In the Property inspector.) The # sign is entered automatically because a hotspot link must begin with a number sign.
5 Edit the Link box to read **#Oregon**	Link #Oregon
	To name the anchor that this hotspot will link to.
Press ↵ENTER	To create a link from the rectangular hotspot to this named anchor.
6 In the Alt box, enter **Oregon**	
Press ↵ENTER	To create alternate text for this hotspot. This will appear as a ScreenTip when a user points to the hotspot.

7 Is the Rectangular Hotspot Tool the most appropriate tool for this hotspot?

   Why or why not?

8 Click

(The Polygon Hotspot Tool is in the Property inspector.) You'll create a polygon hotspot.

9 Point to **NV**, as shown

The pointer changes to a crosshair.

   Click the top-right corner of the state border, as shown

To set the first point of the hotspot polygon.

   Click the top-left corner of the state border, as shown

To define the second point of the polygon. A line appears between the two points.

10 Continue clicking each corner until the hotspot takes the shape of the state, as shown

11 Create a link to the anchor named **#Nevada**

In the Link box, immediately after the number sign, enter Nevada.

12 Create appropriate alternate text for this hotspot

Enter Nevada in the Alt box.

13 Save locations.html

14 Preview the page in your browser

15	Point to **OR**	A ScreenTip with the alternate text appears.
	Click **OR**	To navigate to the named anchor. The page shows the Oregon information.
	Scroll up	(If necessary.) To display the map again.
	Click **NV**	To navigate to the named anchor.
16	Close the browser	
17	Close locations.html	

Topic C: Using CSS link styles

Explanation

By default, text links appear as blue, underlined text. These default styles might suit your Web site's design, but in many cases, blue links don't fit the color scheme of a site. You can use CSS to customize the appearance of links to better fit your site's color scheme. You can also assign styles that act as visual cues to the state of a link.

Link states

Link states define the current condition of a link. There are four link states, as described in the following table.

State	Description
Link	The default state of a link that has not been activated in any way.
Visited	The state of a link after you click it and its destination page has loaded. In many browsers, visited links appear as purple, underlined text by default.
Hover	The state of a link when you point to it. Most browsers do not apply any default formatting to the hover state.
Active	The state of a link when you click it but have not yet released the mouse button. A link is in this state for only a moment. Most browsers do not apply any default formatting to the active state.

Visited links

The browser's cache keeps track of links whose destinations have already been viewed. When a link has been visited, the link remains in that state until the browser's cache is cleared. For example, in Internet Explorer, choose Tools, Internet Options, Clear History to reset the browser's list of visited links.

If you have recently viewed the page that a link references, it will appear in the visited state even if you did not click the link.

Do it!

C-1: Formatting links

Here's how	Here's why
1 Open aboutus.html	You'll set link styles for each state.
2 Select **Home**	
	On the navigation bar.
3 Expand the CSS panel	If necessary.
4 Click [icon]	(The New CSS Rule button is at the bottom of the CSS panel.) The New CSS Rule dialog box appears.
5 Next to Selector Type, click **Advanced**	
In the Selector list, select **a:link**	
Next to Define in, verify that globalstyles.css is selected	
Click **OK**	To create a style for this state and close the dialog box. The CSS Rule Definition dialog box appears.
6 In the Category list, verify that Type is selected	
Click the Color box and select the dark blue color **#000066**	
Under Decoration, check **none**	To remove the underline.
Click **OK**	To format this link state and close the dialog box.
7 Observe the files tab	
	(At the top of the document window.) The CSS file globalstyles.css is open in the background.

8 Create a CSS rule for **a:visited**

Click the New CSS Rule button in the CSS panel. Then, in the New CSS Rule dialog box, select a:visited from the Selector list, and click OK.

Select the dark gray color **#666666**

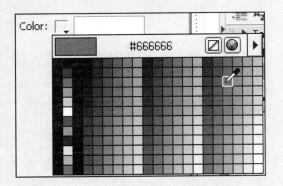

Click the Color box and select the #666666 swatch.

Under Decoration, check **none**

To remove the default underline for the visited state.

Click **OK**

9 Create a CSS rule for **a:hover**

Remove the underline, and give the link state the dark red color **#990000**

10 Create a CSS rule for **a:active**

Remove the underline, and give the link state the dark red color **#990000**

To make the active style the same as the hover style.

11 Observe the CSS panel

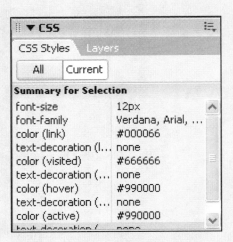

The CSS styles that you created for the link states appear.

12   Activate globalstyles.css

    Observe the styles for the four
    link states

    Save and close globalstyles.css

13   Preview aboutus.html in your
    browser

    Observe the Home link   (In the navigation bar at the top of the page.)
                                        The text appears in the dark blue color that you
                                        specified for links. Any other links that you add
                                        to this page will share this style.

14   Point to **Home**   The text changes to the dark red color you
                                        defined for links in the hover state.

15   Click and hold **Home**   The active state's formatting is the same as the
                                          hover state's formatting.

    Release the mouse button   The browser navigates to the home page,
                                          index.html.

    Click   [⊙ Back ▾]   (In your browser.) To return to aboutus.html.

16   Click a blank area of the page   To deselect the link. The text changes to the
                                          gray color you defined for visited links.

17   Close the browser

    Close aboutus.html

Unit summary: Links

Topic A In this topic, you learned about **links**. You learned about the different link types and targets, and you learned how to create links to pages within a Web site. Then you created **named anchors** and linked to them. Finally, you learned how to create **external links** and **e-mail links**.

Topic B In this topic, you learned how to create an **image map**. You learned how to draw **hotspots** on an image map with various shape tools, and link those hotspots to particular destinations.

Topic C In this topic, you learned about **link states**. You learned that applying styles to link states allows you to fit your links into your color scheme, and gives users information about the links on a page. You learned how to apply CSS styles to each **state**: link, visited, hover, and active.

Independent practice activity

In this activity, you'll create named anchors and link to them, create external links and an e-mail link, and create an image map.

1 From the outlanderspices.com folder in the Practice folder (in the current unit folder), open aboutus.html.

2 Drag a named anchor to the right of the text graphic All Spiced Up, and name it **SpicedUp**.

3 At the top of the table, link the matching text ("All Spiced Up") to this anchor.

4 Create a named anchor for the "Expansion Project" graphic and name it **Expansion**. Link its matching text to this named anchor.

5 Create a named anchor for the "The Project Team" graphic and name it **Team**. Link its matching text to this named anchor. Save aboutus.html, preview the page in your browser, and test the three links.

6 Close the browser and close aboutus.html.

7 Open index.html.

8 For the About Us, Locations, Products, and Recipes items in the navigation bar, create links to their corresponding Web pages. For Contact Us, specify a link to the e-mail address contact@outlanderspices.com. (The page files are in the outlanderspices.com folder in the current unit folder.)

9 Save index.html, and then test the links in your browser.

10 Close the browser and close index.html.

11 Open locations.html.

12 Delete the hotspot for Oregon.

13 Create polygon hotspots for Washington and California, as shown in Exhibit 6-1, and link them to their respective descriptions on that page.

14 Save locations.html, and test the links in your browser.

15 Close the browser and all open files.

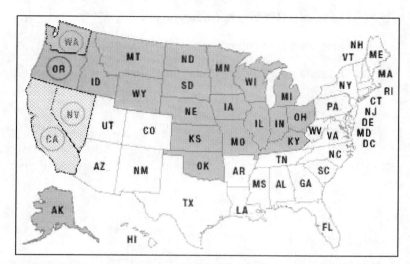

Exhibit 6-1: Image maps for Washington and California after Step 13

Review questions

1 A link with a Self target:

A Opens in a new browser window.

B Opens in an e-mail application.

C Opens in the current browser window.

D Opens in another browser window, only if another browser session is active.

2 A link with a Blank target:

A Opens in a new browser window.

B Opens in an e-mail application.

C Opens in the current browser window.

D Opens in another browser window, only if another browser session is active.

3 Define "hotspot."

4 To create an intra-document link, you need to:

A Create a local link on a page.

B Create a named anchor, and then link to that anchor.

C Create a link from one anchor to another.

D Create a link to a page, and then on that page, create a link back to the original page.

5 The hover state is:

A The default state of a link.

B The state a link enters when you click it.

C The state a link enters when you point to it.

D The state a link enters when it has already been clicked.

Unit 7
Publishing

Unit time: 30 minutes

Complete this unit, and you'll know how to:

A Connect to a Web server with a secure FTP connection, check your site's links, and upload a site.

Topic A: Web site publishing

Explanation

You publish a Web site by copying the site files from your local PC to a remote Web server. A *Web server* is a computer configured with Web server software and the Internet protocols required to serve pages and other resources upon request. Dreamweaver makes it easy to set publishing parameters for your site and to transfer your site files to a Web server.

Publishing basics

A Web server is connected to the Internet via an *Internet service provider* (ISP) or a *hosting center*. The ISP or hosting center provides disk space for Web site files, as well as other services such as site promotion.

Domain names

A *domain name* serves as both the name and address of your site. Your ISP can help you select and register a domain name. For example, a domain name such as www.outlanderspices.com is easy for users to remember, immediately identifies the company, and is fairly easy to type into a browser's address bar.

File names

Your ISP's Web server might run on an operating system that's different from yours and that has different rules for file names. To create file names that comply with just about any operating system, follow these guidelines:

- Keep file names short. For ease of maintenance on the site, the file name should describe the file's content or function.
- Do not include spaces in the name. To separate words, use the underscore character; for example, *product_list.html*.
- Do not use any characters other than letters, numerals, and the underscore.
- Always start file names with a letter.
- Treat uppercase and lowercase letters as different characters. For example, your server might not consider aboutus.html and AboutUs.html to be the same file.

Defining a Web site

To publish files to a Web server, you must first define a Web site on your hard drive. Dreamweaver's Site Definition Wizard makes it easy to move through the setup process.

Do it!

A-1:   Defining a site

Here's how	Here's why
1 Choose **Site**, **Manage Sites...**	To open the Manage Sites dialog box. You'll delete the existing site and create a new one in its place.
Select **outlanderspices.com** and click **Remove**	(If necessary.) To delete any previous site definition. The Macromedia Dreamweaver 8 dialog box appears.
Click **Yes**	To remove the site and close the dialog boxes.
2 Click **New**, **Site**	(In the Manage Sites dialog box.) To start the Site Definition Wizard.
3 Activate the Basic tab	If necessary.
Enter **outlanderspices.com**	To name the Web site.
Click **Next**	
Click **Next**	To confirm that you do not want to use a server technology.
4 Click 📁 and browse to the outlanderspices.com folder	(In the current unit folder.) To specify where the files will be stored.
Click **Select**	To select the folder.
5 Click **Next**	The Sharing Files screen appears.
From the list, select **None**	To specify that there is no remote server connection.
Click **Next**	The Summary screen appears.
Click **Done**	To finish defining the site and close the Site Definition Wizard.

Server connections

Explanation

Before you can upload files to a Web server, you must first establish a connection between your PC and the server. Dreamweaver provides several methods for establishing a connection; one of them is SFTP.

Secure File Transfer Protocol (SFTP) is a popular method of transferring files across the Internet. SFTP uses FTP, the standard file transfer protocol, and combines it with authentication and encryption to protect the transmission (and your data) from unauthorized access.

Before setting up a server connection, check with your ISP to make sure that the Web server supports SFTP. If it does, the ISP typically provides information for connecting to the server; this information includes the FTP host name, the host directory, and a login name and password.

Do it!

A-2: Connecting to a server using secure FTP

Here's how	Here's why
1 Click **Edit**	In the Manage Sites dialog box. You'll explore the steps required to connect to a server through a secure FTP connection. The Site Definition Wizard appears.
2 Activate the Advanced tab	
Under Category, select **Remote Info**	To display the remote connection options.
3 In the Access list, select **FTP**	This page of the wizard is context-sensitive. When you select FTP as the remote connection type, additional fields appear.
4 In the FTP host box, enter **ftp.outlanderspices.com**	To specify the address of an FTP host where files will be sent.
5 In the Host directory box, enter the path to the Test_site folder	(In the current unit folder.) The Host directory specifies the path to the remote site.
6 In the Login box, enter your first name	For a real site, the hosting center administrator would typically assign a user name.
7 In the Password box, enter **password**	For a real site, the hosting center administrator would typically assign a password.
8 Check **Use Secure FTP (SFTP)**	

Access:	FTP
FTP host:	ftp.outlanderspices.com
Host directory:	Test_site
Login:	Lee	Test
Password:	••••••••	☑ Save
	☐ Use passive FTP
	☐ Use firewall	Fire...
	☑ Use Secure FTP (SFTP)

	To encrypt file transfers and guard access to your files, user names, and passwords. The Web server must be an SFTP server.
9 Click **Cancel**	To close the wizard.
Click **Done**	To close the Manage Sites dialog box.

Broken links and orphaned files

Explanation

Before you upload your site files to the Web server, you should verify that all of the links in the site are working correctly. Opening each file and clicking every link, however, would be a tedious task. Fortunately, Dreamweaver can check the integrity of local and external links for you.

Orphaned files

Dreamweaver can also check for *orphaned files*, which are files that reside in your site folders but have no pages linking to them. These files might include early drafts of Web pages or image files that you decided not to use. Removing orphaned files from your site before uploading will prevent unnecessary bloat on the server and make site maintenance easier.

To check links for an entire site:

1　In the Files panel, select a Web site.

2　Right-click in the Files panel and choose Check Links, Entire Local Site.

3　Use the Results panel to identify and repair broken links, as shown in Exhibit 7-1.

4　From the Show list, select External Links to review all external links.

5　From the Show list, select Orphaned Files to display any orphaned files that might exist in your site.

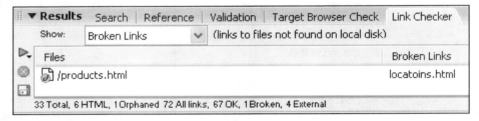

Exhibit 7-1: The Link Checker in the Results panel group

Do it!

A-3: Checking links

Here's how	Here's why
1 In the Files panel, select **Site – outlanderspices.com**	You'll check the links in this site.
2 Right-click in the Files panel and choose **Check Links**, **Entire Local Site**	To check links for all the files in the Web site. The Results panel group appears, with the Link Checker panel activated.
Observe the Broken Links list	A broken link appears in the list. In this case, a typo in the file name breaks the link.
3 Under Broken Links, select **locatoins.html**	
	You'll fix this broken link.
Type **locations.html**	To enter the correct file name for the linked file.
Press (↵ ENTER)	The file no longer appears in the Broken Links list.
4 From the Show list, select **External Links**	To view the external links in this site's pages. These links do not indicate errors; they are listed here for reference only.
5 From the Show list, select **Orphaned Files**	An image file appears. It is not linked to any page in the site. If you move or delete this file, it will not be uploaded to the remote site.
6 Click the Results panel group's title bar	To collapse the panel group.

Under step 3, an illustration shows:

Link Checker   Site Re

Broken Links

locatoins.html

Site publishing

Explanation

When you upload files to a Web server, the local folder where the site resides on your PC is automatically duplicated on the Web server. All files and subfolders are copied.

You can also publish a site to another location on your local PC, either as practice or because your PC is acting as the Web server.

To upload to a local folder:

1 Define a Web site.
2 Choose Site, Manage Sites to open the Manage Sites dialog box.
3 Click Edit to start the Site Definition Wizard.
4 Activate the Advanced tab.
5 Under Category, select Remote Info.
6 In the Access list, select Local/Network. Additional boxes and check boxes appear.
7 Click the Browse button, navigate to the publish folder on your PC or network, and select that folder.
8 Click OK to close the Site Definition Wizard.
9 Click Done to close the Manage Sites dialog box.
10 In the Files panel, click the Put File(s) button.

Do it!

A-4: Uploading a site

Here's how	Here's why
1 Open the Manage Sites dialog box	Choose Site, Manage Sites.
Click **Edit**	You'll practice uploading a site by transferring the site to a folder on your PC.
Activate the Advanced tab	
Under Category, select **Remote Info**	To display the remote connection options.
2 In the Access list, select **Local/Network**	This page of the Site Definition Wizard is context-sensitive. When you select Local/Network as the remote connection type, additional fields appear.
3 Click 🗀	The Browse button.
Navigate to the Test_site folder	In the current unit folder.
Click **Open**	
Click **Select**	To specify this as the remote folder.

4 Click **OK**	The Macromedia Dreamweaver 8 dialog box appears.
Click **OK**	To confirm that a cache will be re-created and to close the dialog box and wizard.
Click **Done**	To close the Manage Sites dialog box.
5 Undock the Files panel group and drag it to the center of the workspace	
6 In the Files panel list, select **Remote view**	
7 Click ▣	(The Expand/Collapse button is in the Files panel.) To view the files in the remote folder in one panel, and the files in the local folder in the other panel.
Click ↻	To refresh the panel and display the remote folder.
8 Click ⬆	To upload the site files from the local folder to the remote folder. The Macromedia Dreamweaver 8 dialog box appears.
Click **OK**	To put (upload) the entire site to the remote folder.
Observe the folders in both panes	Both panes contain the same folders and files.
9 Click ▣	To collapse the Files panel.
10 Dock the Files panel group	Drag the panel group back to the other panel groups.

Unit summary: Publishing

Topic A   In this topic, you learned the basics of **Web site publishing** with Dreamweaver. You learned how to define a site and connect to a server using SFTP. Then you learned how to check for broken links and orphaned files, and review external links. Finally, you learned how to upload a site to a local or remote folder.

Independent practice activity

In this activity, you will define a Web site and check its links.

1 Remove the existing Web site. (*Hint*: Choose Site, Manage Sites, select outlanderspices.com, and click Remove.)

2 Define a new Web site. (*Hint*: Click New, Site to start the Site Definition Wizard. Enter a site name, and browse to the outlanderspices.com folder in the practice folder within the current unit folder.)

3 Check the links in the site. (*Hint*: In the Files panel, right-click the site and choose Check Links, Entire Local Site.)

4 Repair the broken link that was caused by a typo.

5 Observe the external links and orphaned files.

6 Close the Results panel group.

7 Close Dreamweaver.

Review questions

1 It's often wise to choose your site's file names carefully. Which of the following are important guidelines to consider? (Choose all that apply.)

A Keep file names as short and meaningful as possible.

B Start file names with a number.

C Start file names with a letter.

D Do not include spaces in the file names.

E Do not use special characters other than the underscore.

F Separate words in the file names with one space only.

2 What are two advantages of checking your site for orphaned files before uploading it to a remote server?

3 Why might you want to publish to a local folder?

4 What is SFTP?

5 Why is it important to check for broken links before uploading your site?

Course summary

This summary contains information to help you bring the course to a successful conclusion. Using this information, you will be able to:

A Use the summary text to reinforce what you've learned in class.

B Determine the next courses in this series (if any), as well as any other resources that might help you continue to learn about Dreamweaver.

Topic A: Course summary

Use the following summary text to reinforce what you've learned in class.

Unit summaries

Unit 1

In this unit, you learned a few basics about the Internet and HTML. You identified the main components of the **Dreamweaver interface** and learned how to customize the workspace. You also performed **basic Web page editing** by adding and formatting text and images. Finally, you learned about **HTML tags**, including basic structural tags.

Unit 2

In this unit, you **created a Web site**. You also created Web pages and imported text from documents. Finally, you set **page properties**, including page and text color.

Unit 3

In this unit, you learned how to convert line breaks to paragraph breaks and how to separate text into **paragraphs**. Then you learned how to insert **special characters** and spaces. You also learned the basics of **HTML document structure**, and you learned how to create ordered and unordered **lists**. Then you learned the basics of **Cascading Style Sheets (CSS)** and learned about the difference between internal and external style sheets. Finally, you applied element styles and class styles.

Unit 4

In this unit, you learned how to create and format **tables** and nested tables, set row and column properties, insert rows and columns, and apply background color to cells. You also learned how to apply fixed and variable widths, align content in cells, and modify cell borders and cell padding. Finally, you learned how to use a **layout table** and layout cells to design a page layout.

Unit 5

In this unit, you learned about the **GIF**, **JPEG**, and **PNG** image file formats. You learned the advantages and disadvantages of using **image-based text**, and you learned how to modify **image tag attributes** and specify alternate text. Then you learned how to apply image backgrounds and resize images.

Unit 6

In this unit, you learned how to **create links** to other pages and resources, as well as create named anchors and e-mail links. Then you learned how to create **image maps** and draw hotspots by using various shape tools. Finally, you learned about the four **link states** and how to apply CSS styles to each state.

Unit 7

In this unit, you learned how to **connect** to a Web server through a **secure FTP** connection, **check a site for errors** such as broken links and orphaned files, and **upload** a site.

Topic B: Continued learning after class

It is impossible to learn to use any software effectively in a single day. To get the most out of this class, you should begin working with Dreamweaver 8 to perform real tasks as soon as possible. Course Technology also offers resources for continued learning.

Next courses in this series

This is the first course in this series. The next course in this series is:

* *Dreamweaver 8: Advanced*

Other resources

For more information, visit www.course.com.

Dreamweaver 8: Basic

Quick reference

Button	Shortcut keys	Function
		Hides the panel groups and expands the document window.
▽	CTRL + TAB	Expands the Property inspector.
▼		Hides the Property inspector and expands the document window.
I	CTRL + I	Makes the selected text italic.
🌐	F12	Previews the current page in a browser.
Split		Splits the document window into Code view and Design view.
Code		Switches to Code view.
Design		Switches to Design view.
📁		Opens a dialog box where you can browse to a folder.
🗂		Expands and collapses the Files panel.
⊞		Expands a tree in the Files panel or in Map view.
🔗		Attaches an External Style Sheet to the current page.
All		Displays all style-sheet files in the CSS panel.
✏		Opens a style definition (from the CSS panel) for editing.
⊕		Creates a style in the CSS panel.
CSS	SHIFT + F11	Displays the current style-sheet files in the CSS panel, or opens the CSS panel from the Property inspector.

Button	Shortcut keys	Function
	CTRL + ALT + T	Inserts an HTML table when you drag from the button to the document window.
B	CTRL + B	Makes the selected text bold.
	CTRL + ALT + SHIFT + R	Aligns the selected text or object to the right.
		Begins a layout table.
		Begins a layout cell.
		Resets a modified image to its original size and proportions.
	CTRL + ALT + A	Inserts a named anchor in the document.
		Draws a rectangular or square hotspot on an image.
		Draws a polygon hotspot on an image.
	F5	Refreshes the view in the Files panel.
	CTRL + SHIFT + U	Uploads site files from the local folder to a remote folder.

Glossary

Assets

The components of your Web site, such as images or multimedia files.

Cell padding

The amount of space between a cell border and the cell's content.

Class styles

Enable you to give names to your HTML elements. This allows you to define elements and page sections specifically, rather than relying on the default HTML tag names. Class styles can be used multiple times in a document.

Definition list

An HTML list for structuring terms and their corresponding definitions. Often used for glossaries, "frequently asked questions" (FAQs) pages, and similar contexts.

Element styles

CSS styles that define the formatting of HTML elements, such as headings and paragraphs. An element style overrides any default formatting for an HTML element.

External links

Links to a page or resource outside a Web site.

External style sheet

An external text file that's saved with a .css extension and that contains style rules that define how various HTML elements are displayed.

Font set

A set of three or more similar fonts that help ensure consistent text display in a variety of browsers and operating systems.

GIF

An image file format that can support a maximum of 256 colors. GIF files are best used for images with relatively few colors and with areas of flat color, such as line drawings, logos, and illustrations.

HTML

Hypertext Markup Language, the standard markup language on the Web. HTML consists of *tags* that define the basic structure of a Web page.

ID styles

Allow you to create and name your own elements. However, while class styles can apply to multiple elements in a page, ID styles may only be applied to one element per page.

Image map

An image that contains multiple links called *hotspots*.

Internal links

Links to pages or resources within a Web site.

Internal style sheet

One or more style rules embedded in the head section of an HTML document. Styles in an internal style sheet can affect elements in only that document.

Internet

A vast array of networks that belong to universities, businesses, organizations, governments, and individuals all over the world.

JPEG

An image file format that supports more than 16 million colors. JPEG is best used for photographs and images that have many subtle color shadings.

Link states

The various states, or conditions, that a link can be in. There are four link states: link, hover, active, and visited.

Margin

The space between a page's content and the edge of the browser window, and the space between individual elements.

Monospaced font

A typeface in which every character uses the same amount of space; for example, an "i" and an "m" take up the same amount of space on a line. Monospaced fonts (such as Courier) resemble typewriter text.

Named anchor

An element that you identify as an anchor, by naming it, so you can link to it. (Use the Named Anchor dialog box in Dreamweaver, or use the `name` attribute of the `<a>` tag if you're working directly with code.) Also called *bookmark links* or *intra-document links*, named anchors enable you to mark any spot on a page as a target and then link to that target.

Nested list

A list that's inside another list.

Nested table

A table that's inserted in the cell of another table.

Non-breaking space

A special HTML character that inserts a single space without breaking a line.

Ordered list

An HTML list structure that automatically appends sequential labels to each list item. By default, list items are numbered 1, 2, 3, and so on.

Orphaned files

Files that reside in your site folders but are not linked to by any pages. These files might include early drafts of Web pages, or image files that you decided not to use.

PNG

An image file format that combines some of the best features of JPEG and GIF. The PNG format supports more than 16 million colors, and supports many levels of transparency. However, many older browsers do not support the PNG format.

Sans-serif font

A typeface whose characters don't have serifs (flourishes or ornaments at the ends of the strokes that make up the letters).

Serif font

A typeface whose characters have serifs (flourishes or ornaments at the ends of the strokes that make up the letters).

Table cell

The intersection of a row and column in a table. You insert content into table cells.

Unordered list

An HTML list structure that automatically appends bullets to each list item. Use this kind of list when the list items are not sequential and don't need to be in any particular order.

Index

O

P

R

S

T

U

W